Freaks, Geeks and Asperger Syndrome

also by Luke Jackson

A User Guide to the GF/CF Diet for Autism,
Asperger Syndrome and AD/HD
Luke Jackson
Foreword by Marilyn Le Breton
ISBN 978 1 84310 055 3

of related interest

Multicoloured Mayhem
Parenting the many shades of adolescents and children
with autism, Asperger Syndrome and AD/HD
Jacqui Jackson
ISBN 978 1 84310 171 0

Asperger's Syndrome
A Guide for Parents and Professionals
Tony Attwood
Foreword by Lorna Wing
ISBN 978 1 85302 577 8

Pretending to be Normal
Living with Asperger's Syndrome
Liane Holliday Willey
Foreword by Tony Attwood
ISBN 978 1 85302 749 9

Freaks, Geeks and Asperger Syndrome

A User Guide to Adolescence

Luke Jackson

Foreword by Tony Attwood

Jessica Kingsley Publishers
London and Philadelphia

First published in the United Kingdom in 2002
by Jessica Kingsley Publishers
116 Pentonville Road
London N1 9JB, UK
and
400 Market Street, Suite 400
Philadelphia, PA 19106, USA

www.jkp.com

Library of Congress Cataloging-in-Publication Data

Jackson, Luke, 1988-
    Freaks, geeks and asperger syndrome : a user guide to adolescence / Luke Jackson ;
forword by Tony Attwood.
    p. cm.
    Includes index.
    ISBN 1-84310-098-3 (pbk. ; alk. paper)
    I. Jackson, Luke, 1988---Mental health. 2. Asperger's syndrome--Patients--Biography. 3.
Asperger's syndrome--Patients--Family relationships. 4. Asperger's syndrome. 5. Autistic
children. I. Title.

RJ506.A9 J326 2002
618.92'8982'0092--dc21
[B]   2002070930

British Library Cataloguing in Publication Data
A CIP catalogue record for this book is available from the British Library

ISBN 978 1 84310 098 0

Printed and Bound in Great Britain by
Athenaeum Press, Gateshead, Tyne and Wear

Contents

*In memory of Emma-Jane.
So little, so beautiful,
so loved and so missed.*

*If a man does not keep pace with his companions, perhaps it
is because he hears a different drummer. Let him step to the
music he hears, however measured or far away.*
(Henry David Thoreau, 1854)

*To those of you who feel
that you don't belong.
Always remember that different is cool!*

Foreword

At last we have a book for adolescents with Asperger Syndrome, written by a thirteen-year-old who has a diagnosis of Asperger Syndrome. Luke Jackson is an expert on the challenges encountered by his peers. He examines topics that range from the value of a personal explanation of the diagnosis through to experiencing bullying and the dating game. The author has become a mentor to fellow adolescents and writes as though he is having a conversation with the reader. The research evidence on Asperger Syndrome suggests that such individuals have difficulty conceptualizing the thoughts and feelings of other people, yet Luke has a clear insight into the thoughts of fellow adolescents and the concerns of parents and teachers. He also has a distinct sense of humour that will appeal to fellow adolescents.

The chapters include explanations and strategies that are not available in other texts. Luke explains the importance of having a diagnosis and adopts a very positive attitude; he writes 'I have what some people would call a disability but I call a gift'. His analogies and descriptions are unique. He covers topics such as fascinations and fixations, sensory perception, diet, sleep, teenage language, problems with socializing at school, homework, dealing with bullies, the do's and don'ts of dating, moral dilemmas and an explanation of idioms that are particularly confusing for those with Asperger Syndrome. My reactions on reading the manuscript ranged from admiration of his ability to describe the typical life experiences with an eloquence that is quite remarkable, to recognizing the value of his recommendations that will be of considerable benefit to parents, teachers and professionals. I will now benefit by incorporating Luke's wisdom into my clinical work.

The book is dedicated 'to those of you who feel that you don't belong. Always remember that different is cool.' Adolescents with Asperger Syndrome who have low self-esteem, sometimes feel anxious, depressed and annoyed will find that Luke's book becomes an emotional restorative. His style is entertaining and educational but I would add that it is also therapeutic. This book will enhance our understanding of Asperger Syndrome, change attitudes and replace bleak despair with insight and laughter.

Tony Attwood
May 2002

Acknowledgements

Although people with Asperger Syndrome like routines and familiarity, and I am no different, I am aware that to be predictable in the way I write and what I say would be boring to those of you who are reading this book, especially those of you who have already read my other book.

Even so I still have to thank a few people and this seems as good a place to say them as any. So any of you who have heard it all before, please bear with me.

- First, I'd like to give a big thank you and a round of applause to my Mum (AKA Superwoman) for helping me so much with this book and life in general.

- To Jessica, my publisher, for not only helping me with my book but also for being a good friend.

- To Sarah, Anna and Rachel for giving me a hand with the…ahem…dating chapter of the book.

- To Matthew, Joseph and Ben for merely being such good brothers. Thanks for all the fun we have together.

- To Marilyn le Breton for inspiring me and encouraging me to do the gluten-free/casein-free (GF/CF) diet. Without it I wouldn't be where I am today.

- To Paul Shattock whose unfailing research enabled me to feel so much better. (Sorry, Paul. I missed you out of my last book!)

- To Julia Leach for making me realize that I am not a freak.

- To Master Waddington, my Taekwondo instructor. Thank you for my new-found confidence and co-ordination.

1

An Introduction – Me and My Family

My name is Luke Christopher Jackson. I have brown – though a lot of the time greasy – short hair. I have it spiked with gel at the moment. You can see a picture of it on the back of the book. I have greenish blue eyes, which look like the sea. Mum says they are 'deep' though I know this does sound rather ridiculous – the eye is only as deep as from the cornea to the eye socket. I am often told that I am deep too. This means that I think a lot. I am quite small for my age, but so are all the rest of my family too. I think it must be in our genes.

I would like to think that I am helpful and quite kind. I am very polite; I think that is very important.

I have written this book for many reasons. As I have got older and become a teenager I have been asking all sorts of questions and encountering a whole new set of difficulties. I searched and searched the internet for books to answer my questions and there were none – none that were specifically for adolescents. There were plenty of books about adolescence, but not for people like me (I will explain why I am different in a moment). I like writing and I like to be helpful, so I hope that in writing a book myself I will have answered some questions that other adolescents are asking and at the same time helped parents and carers to understand their child more. Another big reason for writing this was the hope that professionals of any sort may read it and begin to understand the many, many people who are similar to me.

So, if you are a professional, don't just put this down and think that I am a sweet kid. Please read on and learn more. I hope very much to entertain you whilst you are learning!

Before I do write more about myself though, I would like to tell you a little about my family. I think we are all pretty interesting. My family consists of seven children and my Mum. These are (in chronological order) Mum – obviously we just call her Mum but her real name is Jacqueline Carol; Matthew Richard – he is eighteen; Rachel Louise – she is sixteen; Sarah Elizabeth – she is fourteen; me, I became thirteen recently; Anna Rebekah – she is eleven; Joseph David – he is eight; and Ben Curtis – he is five.

My big brother Matthew's lifelong ambition is to join the Marines. This is so ironic because Mum never liked guns, toys or otherwise. We have never had toy guns in our house and now Matthew is going off to sea cadets each week and polishing real ones! Matthew was born really early and weighed less than 'a bag of sugar' (everyone always says that). When Ben was born and we all used to go and see him in the special care baby unit, the nurses there used to say to each other 'Do you remember Matthew? He was a twenty-four-weeker.' What a strange expression! It meant that he was born at twenty-four weeks. He is dyslexic and dyspraxic, which means clumsy. Boy, is he clumsy! He has great big feet, which are usually clad in clumpy army boots. He stoops over and resembles a troll banging about. All he needs is a big club over his shoulder and the picture would be complete! We get on well most of the time. He is a good big brother and we have fun together.

Rachel is very talented in many ways, in fact all ways. There is nothing Rachel cannot do. She is very sociable and popular, especially with the boys! Rachel sings and sings and sings. She says she wants to be a singer and she has a really good voice but I have to admit that it gets on my nerves. One thing that she is really outstanding at is art, particularly drawing. Some of her drawings are amazing and that is a huge compliment coming from me as sometimes she really annoys me. I suppose that is because she is the complete opposite of me and so we don't understand each other so well.

Sarah is talented too, but in a quiet way. She is a brilliant dancer. She was a dancing chicken in a school play recently and she surpassed everyone else in that! Sarah has a lot of funny ways and the most hilarious thing about it is that she doesn't even know! She seems to have a hearing problem. Mum says to her, 'Can you make a cup of tea please Sarah?' and Sarah looks at her meaningfully and says 'Ooh'. That is her answer to most things. She seems a complete airhead but yet I know that she thinks a lot and works hard. At school she is very quiet. She is actually a lot like me. She takes things *very* literally and beware anyone who accidentally prods her or touches her – she does not like her space invaded!

Anna is going to be more like Rachel I think. She is popular and tries a bit too hard to be grown up. She is a very good dancer too. One thing Anna is really talented at is writing poems. She can just think them up so quickly. I think one day she will get some of hers published. She has written quite a few about my brothers and me. She is very good at looking after Ben and I think she is more responsible with him than anyone else in the family (apart from Mum, of course). She's like a little mother. Anna likes food, especially sweets, and that is the bottom line – that describes Anna! She is actually very good to have around for us at the moment because she likes to bake and is trying out new things all the time. She makes some really good gluten- and casein-free (that's a special diet we're on that I'll tell you more about later) concoctions. Maybe she will be a chef when she gets older.

Joseph has great problems listening and is hyperactive. He is never still and jumps and cartwheels everywhere. That has been a lot better recently though he still has serious problems listening and concentrating; AD/HD it's called. That is attention deficit, hyperactivity disorder. Since he has been on this special diet he has had quite a lot of the 'H' taken out of the AD/HD but not so much of the 'A'. The school he is at try hard to help him and find ways for him to listen and concentrate.

At the school I go to now, there is a boy in my class who acts just like Joe. He is really silly and, to be honest, very funny a lot of the time. Joe is hilarious in his antics. This boy doesn't listen either and does the most daft, impulsive things. I later found out that he has AD/HD and things just clicked into place in my mind. He was most definitely the same as Joe though a lot 'naughtier'.

Joe has the wildest imagination of anyone I have ever met. I think he would be great as a storywriter. The only thing with this is that when he tells other people his 'stories' no one ever knows which are his fantasies and which are reality. I sometimes wonder whether Joe knows either! Mum gets very worried about this sometimes because he is so believable that if he told someone something bad, other people may believe him.

I remember being with Mum when she picked him up from school a few years ago and his support worker brought him out. 'Hello Joe, have you had a good day?' Mum said cheerily. 'Oh yes thank you,' said Joe. 'My teacher didn't hit me once today.' His poor teacher went scarlet and even Mum looked shocked. If people on the autistic spectrum have problems with imagination then that certainly describes Joe – it is a real impairment not being able to work out where the line between reality and fantasy is!

Last of all is Ben. He was born very early too and had a brain haemorrhage, which caused his muscles to have problems. He used to jerk his legs about in his sleep and his body would arch backwards. It took over two-and-a-half years for him to learn to sit up. He can walk now at last though he is not very confident. He would love to be able to jump but no way can he do that. I feel sorry for him as he wobbles about when he tries to run. He kind of 'fast walks' with his head lolling to the side, looking as if his body is trying to catch up with it. When we go out, if he is not familiar with a place, he just crawls.

Ben is also autistic and can be a complete nutter at times. All he used to do was line things up and flick his fingers in front of his face. We are all on a special diet (as I have said, I have written more about this later on in the book) and Ben has changed a lot since then. He is now an 'active but odd' autistic person instead of the 'locked into his own world' kind of autistic person that he was before.

Ben has massive problems with his senses. Everything seems to be extreme with him. He spends so much time with his fingers in his ears and now he can talk better, he shouts 'too noisy' for almost everything. He also hates wearing clothes and if he does, he has to have the labels cut out. He can spot a label a mile off. Mum has done all sorts of desensitizing stuff with Ben for years and he can now touch grass and dry sand and even put up with paint after a while. These things need to be helped as much as possible because no one can spend his life with his fingers in his ears.

Ben has a lot of trouble understanding what other people are talking about but the difference since the diet is that now he wants to. He goes up to people and licks them or sings 'slim shady' in their face. He is very hard to understand and doesn't talk so well so this is very funny to watch, but I feel quite sorry for him actually. He is so confused most of the time. He is absolutely unbelievably good on the PlayStation. So much better than Mum – but then that wouldn't be hard!

As you can see, we are quite a mix of ages and personalities. Although we get on each other's nerves sometimes and often argue, we have fun too.

I am very interested in commonly used expressions that seem to make very little sense. They are called idioms. Ones that spring to mind in relation to my family are 'Too many cooks spoil the broth' and 'Many hands make light work'. Rather than explain what each expression means throughout the book, I will make a list of the ones I have used and their meanings in the back. It's a good ploy to ensure that you read on, too! So if I write some obscure sentence in the middle of a chapter – turn to the back of the book.

2

Asperger Syndrome and the Autistic Spectrum

After reading a little about my family, you may be thinking, 'OK, fairly interesting, but not enough to write a book about.' Well I will now tell you in more detail why I have done so.

One unusual thing about me is that I have what some people would call a disability but I call a gift – Asperger Syndrome (AS). I know there are many books written about Asperger Syndrome and quite a few from people who actually have it, but I am hoping that writing about myself and my perspective on life may help other people to understand themselves or their children better. I am only thirteen so my view on life may be different from an adult. Then again it may not. Mum always says I am thirteen going on thirty. That means that she thinks I talk and act as if I am older than I really am.

Although I am a teenager and have Asperger Syndrome, I would hope that my book will help people who are younger and older than me and also those who are anywhere on the autistic spectrum, not just those with Asperger Syndrome. Although people on the autistic spectrum are very different, there are also many similarities in the way we think and perceive the world. I know this because of my brothers.

I do like to be helpful and I especially like the idea of helping other kids on the autistic spectrum. If there are any teenagers or adolescents reading this, then I know how hard it is to stand out from the crowd, but yet so desperately want to blend in. Please read on and I will give you all the tips I can. I know I am a boy (stating the obvious rather here!) and so have written from my perspective, but AS girls or parents and carers of AS girls, don't think this stuff doesn't apply. I am sure that a lot is relevant.

Here's a bit of stuff that explains what AS is, but not in too much detail because that isn't what this book is about. There are loads of others that do that. Take a look at the Further Reading section. Asperger Syndrome comes under the umbrella of autism. That's quite a useful way to think of the autistic spectrum – as an umbrella with lots of people under it all in different places. The trouble with that analogy is that some people are being rained on a lot harder than others and that doesn't really happen with an umbrella.

Sarah

It never rains but it pours. The talk of umbrellas reminded me of this expression but it actually has very little to do with autism; I just have a 'grasshopper mind'. I am not sure that any analogy can accurately describe the variety of people who have some kind of autism so I am not going to bother comparing it any more.

AS is usually described as a mild form of autism but, believe me, though the good outweighs the bad, there are some bits that most certainly are not mild. AS people reading this, do you feel as if you only have a 'mild' problem when you are having one of those days where you feel as if you may well be from another planet?

Some people call it a communication disorder too. In some ways I suppose that is accurate because, although we communicate with others, wires seem to get crossed and they get the wrong messages. The same goes the other way. Other people's interactions and communications with us somehow get distorted in transit.

Sorry AS people, if I am being rather cryptic here. I hate it when people talk like that and here I am doing it myself – I am writing a book though! Just try to think of a telephone wire going from us to non-AS people and as the words travel down the wires, they jumble up and get distorted.

Anyway here is what other books say about autism and Asperger Syndrome. Apparently for both autism and Asperger Syndrome, people have a 'triad of impairments'. I only know bits about this from what I have read (and from personal experience, of course). These impairments are in communication, social interaction and imagination. Repetitive behaviours, obsessions and sensory problems are also often part of the problem, though not always present. Mum told me that she read somewhere that someone compared these problems with an equalizer and all people on the autistic spectrum have different levels for each problem. I think this is a really good analogy so whoever you are that thought of it, thank you!

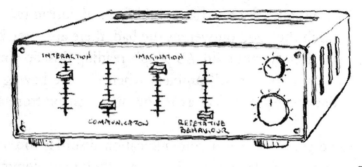

Sarah

The problems with communication, social interaction and imagination affect everyone differently. Some people on the lower end of the autistic spectrum may not talk at all, whilst others with AS or high functioning autism (HFA) seem to speak rather differently and have difficulties understanding a lot of other forms of communication such as facial expressions and body language. These things can be learned to a certain extent I think, though we will probably not see things as the majority see them (nor would we want to!).

Apparently I am very pedantic and speak slowly and monotonously. My sisters often tell me stuff like this! I am also told that I have a problem with communication because I do not know when I am boring someone. I suppose this is true. I like to talk about computers and don't usually realize that others don't want to. Well actually I do, but when I am thinking about computers I am not thinking about anyone else.

Problems with social interaction can be so, so varied. Poor or no eye contact is seen to be a problem with social interaction, though I would dispute that. It is only a problem for those who want to be looked at.

Ben has real problems with social interaction, but if someone came into our house they wouldn't realize this, as he is quite sociable and relaxed there. When he is out, he goes up to people and licks their feet or grins right into their faces and keeps saying, 'What's your name?' However many times they answer, he keeps grinning and saying the same thing over and over again.

Joe too has a problem with social interaction but certainly not in the way I do. He goes up to strangers and chats to them and tells them our life story and asks all sorts of personal questions and says things which I know that others consider rude. We recently had our feet measured at a shoe shop and when the lady asked Joe a question he ignored her. She repeated it again and he said, 'Oh sorry I didn't know you were talking to me as you are very cross-eyed' (which she was).

I am just illustrating how these problems with communication and social interaction can be so different from person to person and through all areas of the autistic spectrum. AS people often find it difficult to mix and can't quite fathom out what they are meant to do when with other people. In our area the autism team have started an AS social club and we laughed because it seemed such a contradiction in terms. The funny thing is that though we are all varied in our abilities, our interests are all pretty much the same so we can talk about computers incessantly and be accepted. It's good to know that I am in a group of people like myself. Because I have adapted fairly well and, though I don't like to boast (snigger from my sisters here!), I am fairly intelligent, I wonder if anyone realizes how hard and tiring life is sometimes. It's such a break to be sat in a group of people who all know that I do have genuine difficulties.

Repetitive behaviours speak for themselves – of course they don't speak but I mean the term is self-explanatory! People often flap their hands or do things that may seem weird to other people. These are all very satisfying and comforting things to do actually, but generally not accepted in our wonderful world. I tend to think of it as a bit like playing with your privates or picking your nose (if you excuse me being so blunt). If you are going to do it then don't do it in public. Of course, if these are involuntary things, then that is different. Personally it doesn't bother me who flaps and jumps. All this stuff is about 'appearing normal' and really no one should ever have to do that, but if you do want to fit in, then there is no harm in trying to blend in as long as it isn't a strain and you don't try to pretend to be something that you are not.

People differ in the way all these problems affect them and the way they deal with them. We are not clones and all have different personalities, appearances and behaviours. Some people are also far better at 'pretending to be normal' than others and some people prefer not to. I try to find a balance between making an effort to mix with others without standing out too much, and accepting the inevitable – that I am always going to seem a little different. I am not sure whether I do a good job of this.

A label or a signpost?

A lot of people worry about whether it is a good thing to actually give someone's problems a name (and I don't mean Bob or Fred!). By this I mean actually getting a proper diagnosis of Asperger Syndrome or autism or whatever someone has, instead of it just being called complex difficulties or global developmental delay or something like that.

Many doctors and a lot of people seem to think that if someone's difficulties actually have a name, then they become a reality and people might actually start to live up to them. I think a lot of people also think a label is a bad thing and will make others automatically conjure up negative ideas if they hear the word 'autistic'. It is possible that these doctors and therapists may have the person's best interest at heart and think that maybe as they get older people might not want to give them a job if they have a syndrome or a 'disability'.

Even if doctors are being well meaning, I still think that is wrong. If someone got a job and behaved oddly or could not cope with some things, they would get the sack (isn't that a strange expression?), but if someone knew that it was part of a problem they could just help them to overcome it and realize they were still capable of good work. Disability Acts now mean that employers are not allowed to discriminate against disabled people, and AS is counted as a disability even though lots of us (I am throwing in a dash of arrogance and including myself in that category!) are more than able in many ways.

Hands up those of you reading this who have been called a freak or a geek or a boffin or a nerd? (Or any variation on this theme!) I am pretty sure that would be the majority of AS kids, probably adults too. Do any of you actually feel freaky on the inside? Here, I will raise my hand and sing out a resounding 'Ay' (that means 'yes' in Old English).

Doctors, therapists and professionals in general, this is how we feel when we do know what the reason is. When we didn't know and didn't have a diagnosis (or weren't told about it) it was a million times worse than you can ever imagine.

If the child you are seeing has one or two boxes of the checklist you are working from still unchecked, then please for the sake of their sanity, tell them or their parents if you have any suspicion that they have AS. After all, as we get older and understand ourselves better, then maybe more and more bits of the AS are not so glaringly obvious.

I think Tony Attwood wrote about labels being signposts (see Further Reading at the end of the book). Signposts usually point people in the right direction, so by not telling people about AS, no direction is being given about how to help.

Sarah

This is *so* unfair to everyone. I think that all the therapy and support at school is a lot harder to get if a child has no diagnosis. Surely the child must stand a better chance of improving in every way if everyone knows what their problem is and how best to help?

Many people can struggle on for years and years without ever getting a diagnosis of anything at all. I am one of the lucky ones who got answers to the questions Mum was asking (though she didn't tell me!). No one wants to have a syndrome and no one wants to tell people that they have got one, so sometimes things get left unsaid or not even thought of in the first place. This is not the best way at all. Diagnosing someone, which can actually answer a lot of questions, must be hard both for doctors and parents. After all, how does anyone actually decide what a problem is? No checklists could ever cover the subtle ways some problems affect us and a good doctor or therapist must surely be one who realizes that.

If someone is older then they must be quite sure themselves that there is something different about them and the doctors should listen very carefully. If the parent is telling a doctor that they think their child has AS or autism, then there must be a very good reason for this. Why would any parent want their child to have anything wrong with them?

Of course a lot of people will not have heard of AS so cannot possibly suspect that their child or they themselves have it. Even with much more use of the internet, there will still be people without internet access and people who do not read much. So here the problem lies. If the doctor doesn't know enough to diagnose properly and the parent or person doesn't know at all, then everyone is left scratching their heads and wondering why they or their child are having so many problems. The answer to this is that doctors need to learn in more detail about the Asperger Syndrome and autism and listen to those of us who actually live with it.

I think what we have here is a Catch-22 situation – if the world in general does not understand or accept that people are all different, then people with AS are reluctant to tell others about it for fear of being considered a freak. After all, no one wants to be treated as if they have some contagious disease. These things then go unmentioned and people stay nervous and uncomfortable around someone who is seen to have a disability, especially when it is an invisible one. The people with the disability learn to keep quiet and struggle on; the doctors and the rest of the world therefore learn nothing – and so it goes on!

This is rather like the last episode of *Star Trek Voyager*, 'Endgame', in that when the future version of Captain Janeway went back into the past to save the past version of Captain Janeway from the Borg and near the end got herself assimilated by the Borg queen herself. This episode had a strange twist to it – the future version of Captain Janeway would grow up, go into the past, save the past version of Captain Janeway from the Borg and then get assimilated herself and so it would go on in a never ending cycle.

Luke

I would like to think that this circle of silence and lack of understanding could be broken by a few people and then there could be more setting the ball rolling and talking about the real stuff that goes on in the mind of someone with Asperger Syndrome, and also making others, especially doctors, realize that we don't all fit into a carefully planned set of rules. To me that is rigid thinking on the doctor's part!

There are now professionals – Tony Attwood for one – who spend loads of time bothering to properly learn and write books on AS and try to inform others. Then there are adults with AS: Liane Holiday Willey is one, who writes about her own experiences. This should help adults, who maybe are undiagnosed, to get to know themselves better. Kenneth Hall is a child who has written about this life and AS and was only ten when he wrote it. I would hope that my books would help parents and professionals and AS kids all understand better too.

As people get older, they often get better at disguising their problems and fitting into the world. Who was it that said 'No man is an island'? I know that is stating the obvious and of course no man is an island, but it means that no one lives totally alone without any rules or society somewhere about them. I did think that I may not the best person to write a book on how someone with AS thinks, as I thought that a lot of AS traits had been eradicated. However, this teenage stuff is making me have a rethink and also I don't think Mum and my brothers and sisters fully agree anyway! I can't comment too much on that because I am me.

The best advice I would give to parents that have found out that their child has AS is just to accept them as they are. Preconceived ideas are never a good thing. To be on the autistic spectrum is not the same as being on death row – it is not a death sentence, it is not terminal, it is merely a name for a lifelong set of behaviours. Yours and your child's life may now take a different course than you would have expected, but it is just as important and may even be more fascinating and enlightening. Reading books and learning lots about it is good (I wouldn't bother writing one otherwise), but don't think that they have somehow changed because they have a name for their behaviours. Your kid is still your kid regardless of his or her label.

3
To Tell or Not to Tell?

Giving the news

A lot of parents find it difficult to tell their child that they have Asperger Syndrome (or whatever they may have). I suppose there are many reasons for this and parents probably think that sometimes it is in a child's best interest not to tell them. Some parents may just not get round to telling them. Maybe they are always waiting for the right time but, whatever the reasons, I personally think that a child *should* be told and the sooner the better. Believe me I know!

I know I have said this already but I cannot stress this point enough. Doctors and professionals who can give a diagnosis, this is where not giving one causes a *big* problem. Please don't think I am being cheeky or telling you your job; I am just telling it like it is from the inside. You may think that if the child or person you are seeing has lots of AS traits but you can't fit them neatly into your checklist of criteria, then you are doing them a favour by saying that they haven't got it. In fact it doesn't make them not have AS. It just muddles them up more and makes them and all around them think that they are even more 'freakish'.

A parent is not likely to tell a child that he or she has AS if the doctors or professionals don't agree. You will not be upsetting or

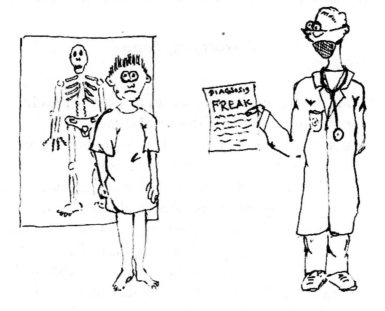

Rachel

worrying the family any more than they already are. They will be relieved, not because something is wrong, just because they know what it is and so how to face it. So be one of those few and far between doctors who actually recognize that AS exists in many forms. Thanks to any of you who are taking notice!

I was one of the ones who found out later rather than sooner and it took the arrival of an autistic brother to push Mum into telling me. I think that happens with a lot of people. I know loads of families where there is one AS kid and also a younger more severely autistic kid too. This is how I found that I had AS and believe me this way is *not* ideal. Still – all's well that ends well! (Sorry about the cliché!)

A Worrying Time

One day we all went out for tea to a pub – I really don't like the sound of that word – some onomatopoeic words are really cool but pub sounds like it should be one of those but it isn't!

This place had a children's play area outside with climbing frames and slides and stuff. There were wood shavings on the floor to act as some kind of cushioning in case a child falls. I actually hate these wood shavings because they get everywhere. I don't particularly like places like that either but I usually get forced to 'go and play' so I find some way to occupy myself and please Mum at the same time. AS kids – it can be done! Of course now I am a cool teenager so all I need to do is stand around and pose. I am not sure what that entails but it is easier than having to climb and get messy!

Mum had asked Rachel to take Ben to play, although Ben just didn't play at all at that time. He couldn't walk and giggled hysterically most of the time. He could sit up though, so she sat him on the wood shavings and he just stayed put, picking up wood shavings and putting them into some kind of pile. He was totally oblivious to the fact that there were children running around him, in fact he was oblivious to everything. Rachel then came over to Mum and said out of the blue, 'Did you know that Ben is autistic?' Mum said, 'Thank you, Doctor Jackson' and ignored her. But I didn't ignore her. I asked why she had said that. Rachel said that a long time before she had seen a poster on the wall of the child development centre which said 'Autism is…' and listed things. Ben did every single one of these things.

When Ben was a bit older and started to put things in and out of boxes for ages (including him) and line things up and cling tightly onto a Chinese cookery book for no apparent reason, everyone, me included, was silently or not so silently comparing him to me. There were so many similarities though of course he couldn't talk and walk and I could! This was quite an uncomfortable time for me and probably everyone else, because watching Ben was like watching a video of me played back and then exaggerated. Still no one mentioned it though!

At this time I began to suspect that I had something wrong with me too. So many of Ben's ways were similar to mine when I was young. There was one confusing thing about this though. I was very aware of everything about me, could talk fine from the right age and I certainly didn't use to giggle hysterically – apparently I never stopped screaming! This was a very worrying and confusing time for me and to be honest I thought I was going mad.

When Ben was having the usual assessment with the educational psychologist, Julia Leach, Mum told me later that Julia convinced her that it was unfair to leave me wondering why I was so much like Ben – talk about an understatement! Phew – thanks Julia!

If anyone is wondering when to tell their child that they have AS, then in my humble opinion, the answer is *right now*!

I first found out I had Asperger Syndrome, therefore, from an article in *The Guardian* that Julia gave Mum to show me. It was all about Asperger Syndrome and about how Albert Einstein was supposed to have had it. It told how many people with Asperger Syndrome had been very successful in their lives. One of those people was Bill Gates, the director of Microsoft. Although these weren't actually diagnosed, they were recognized to have 'traits' of AS. The article had a checklist of certain behaviours that were considered to be traits of Asperger Syndrome.

I was twelve years old when I read this article. Mum had just plonked it in front of me as if she had done it by accident. She knows that I read everything and anything. As I read through the article my first reaction was relief. It was if I had a weight lifted off my shoulders. I had every single 'symptom' on this checklist. I read it and reread it, then said to Mum, 'Do you think I could have AS?' She simply said, 'Yes, you have.' I must admit I did think, 'Well thanks a lot for telling me', but the relief was most definitely stronger than the annoyance (at that time anyway).

I had finally found the reason why other people classed me as weird. It was not just because I was clumsy or stupid. My heart lightened instantly and the constant nagging that accompanied me all my life (not my Mum) stopped immediately. I finally knew why I felt different, why I felt as if I was a freak, why I didn't seem to fit in. Even better, it was not my fault! At first I wanted to run out and tell the world. I felt like charging out into the streets and shouting, 'Hey, look at me, I have Asperger Syndrome. I am not a freak.' But as usual logic just took over – if I did that there would be a number of drawbacks. First, I would be in big trouble! Running out into the street is something that I am not allowed to do. Second, at the time I had my pyjamas on so I would have been cold. Third, no one in our street even knows me so they wouldn't think I was a 'freak' anyway.

I will elaborate a bit more about this. A lot of people who don't know that I have Asperger Syndrome say that I am a freak. Come to think of it, a lot of people who do know that I have AS call me a freak! I suppose that is because I am not your average child. I like to think of myself as the 'new and improved model' (this is a huge compliment to all AS people reading this book!), but I don't think most other people would agree with me. I reckon some people might even say the opposite – that I was defective in some way. A 'freak', by the way, seems to be anyone who doesn't act, look or speak like the rest of the world. The *Oxford Dictionary* says that a freak is:

1. a person or thing that is abnormal in form;

2. something very unusual or irregular;

3. a person who dresses absurdly;

4. one who freaks out, i.e. a drug addict.

Well, aren't those open to interpretation?! What on earth is normal, usual or regular anyway? This of course comes back to the majority ruling, I reckon. Number four is quite strange because later on I will explain how in many autistic people, gluten and casein produce the effect of morphine and make people on the autistic spectrum become addicted.

I know I am being repetitive but I will emphasize my point again. This is an important chapter for parents to read because I can't stress enough how bugged I was to 'discover' my AS at least five years after I was actually diagnosed. Mum could have saved me a lot of years of worry because I always knew I was different. When I was asking Mum why she had not told me for such a long time about AS, she said that she was bothered that I may read up on it and start to experience 'symptoms' that I didn't actually have. I think this was very stupid! I do wonder whether she thought I would grow out of it too.

After I had been told about AS, quite a few questions were in my mind and maybe they are in yours if you are reading this and have just found out. The first thing I wanted was proof. Where could I get to get a blood test? Who was it that decided I had AS and how did they know? The answer to the first one is that there is no blood test, brain scan or anything that will actually prove or disprove AS. You may have these things just to check you have nothing else, but mostly they show nothing.

If you have already been diagnosed, then doctors or speech therapists or psychologists will probably have done all sorts of tests and asked questions to your school and family to work out why and if you think differently. Sometimes, you may know yourself that you have AS but doctors and professionals may not. I have explained about that earlier. The important thing is that you know and accept for yourself that you are different. After all, you know yourself best!

The next thing I wanted to know was if there is a cure. Well, sorry if you don't like this answer, but no there most definitely is not. For those of us that have learned to accept our differences this is a very good thing. To cure someone of AS would be to take away their personality and some really cool abilities too.

As I have mentioned and will go into more detail about later, my brothers and I are on a special diet. This is not to cure AS or autism, but for many others and for us, the diet really helps some of the bad bits. There are many different therapies for AS and autism and some help some people and some help others.

Kenneth Hall wrote his book *Asperger Syndrome, the Universe and Everything* and talked a lot about applied behavioural analysis

(ABA). This is a form of therapy where you work for rewards for positive behaviour. This wouldn't work for me but it did for him and others. I have included links about that at the back of the book. I am just highlighting the fact that there are many different therapies available and what is good for one person is not good for another. These aren't looking for cures; they are looking for ways to make life easier.

Although a child may go through this period of asking questions or being angry and upset, in my mind that is still no excuse not to tell them. Parents, you are not protecting them because feeling as if you are a 'freak' is horrible at any time and much worse when you don't know the reasons why.

I don't know whether I can be considered to be qualified to advise people about how to deal with their children as I am only a child myself (even though someone said – I can't remember who – that the best experts on AS are the people with AS themselves), but if I can give any advice at all I would say that it is much better to bring up the child so they know and accept at an early age that they are different from other people and why. If it is talked about quite easily and casually, then they will just accept that AS or whatever is part of them and they are unique and special.

If the child gets taken to see doctors and other people and the parents talk in whispered conversations about them and tell the child nothing, then that is denying the child the right to know about themselves. Assessments are also perfect opportunities to tell a child that they have AS. Most of us kids with something different about us get used to performing tests and being asked questions and because we don't socialize the same, we never do realize that this isn't something that every child does throughout their life. This is *very* unfair! So my final word on this subject is *get them told!*

How and when to tell other people

When I was writing this I was trying to think of a catchy subheading. As you can see I didn't manage it! One thing that I did come up with though was 'coming out of the closet'. This made me laugh because it is the expression that people use when they are going to tell others that they are homosexual. It is a really funny expression anyway. After all, if someone really was stuck in a closet then others wouldn't automatically think that they were gay! In some ways, homosexual people must have the same worries as those with AS, when it comes to telling others that they are different from others.

Rachel

There are a lot of difficulties when it comes to deciding whom to tell about the fact that you have AS. I mean, can you imagine what a good chat-up line that is? 'Hi babe, I'm Luke and I have Asperger

Syndrome.' Somehow I think her reaction to that would be 'run away'. (Don't you just love Monty Python?!) I know some people would say that if learning such a thing puts someone off then they are not worth knowing anyway. That is not so easy to accept when the person in question is a particularly fit member of the opposite sex! Personally, I reckon that if someone already knows you and accepts you, then it is easier to tell them. Obviously I am speaking as a teenager (I have a knack for stating the obvious!) and this may be different for different ages.

Sometimes it just isn't realistic to say that we shouldn't bother with people who change their attitudes once they discover that you have AS. That person may be someone whom you just have to spend time with, whether you like it or not. A teacher is a good example of this. In some ways all teachers need to know is that a child has a problem in certain areas. After all, if they don't know, they can't help. This is very true in infant or junior school. In my opinion, things change when you get to senior school. Teachers are people – some good and some bad (in fact some seem to be downright sadists) – and maybe it is not a good thing for all to know straight away that you have a problem. Some teachers are just nasty and will jump at the chance of making fun of someone.

All this gets very tricky! The very heart of AS is that we are not able to decipher other people's thoughts, feelings and motivations – we can't put ourselves 'in their shoes' (if you saw some of my teachers, believe me you definitely wouldn't want to – phew!). Because of this problem it really does make it very difficult to know who is likely to be helpful and supportive and who is likely to make things worse either by accident or on purpose. I can't work that out at all so I usually just keep my mouth shut and hope that Mum sorts stuff like that out. After all I am only thirteen so I may get better at working out this stuff as I get older.

Some people may be born campaigners and tell everyone instantly that they have AS and are proud of it. Here comes another similarity to gay people. These are actually the kind of people who get things changed in the world and fight for rights of minority groups and lots of people should be thankful to them.

I suppose I am doing my bit by writing of my own experiences in the hope that it will help others and enlighten them. But at least with a book I can be selective about who I tell about it and who not. I think it is very brave to go parading around telling everyone about things that a lot of people would rather not know and may even persecute you for, but this is where we are all different. My way and my view is just to try and mix with people as best as I can and if people don't like me for who I am then they can just like it or lump it and no explanations are needed.

With teachers, again it is a bit different and in general most teachers try hard to understand when they realize I am different from the other kids. In most schools, the teachers will know anyway. At some point, there is often a time when there is no way that I can hide that fact that something is causing me a problem – games is an obvious example. In this situation it is really important that the teacher knows why something is so difficult, even if they don't seem to give a damn anyway!

As I get older, people of my age are developing more of their own personalities, or trying to. At least I am not expected to participate in mindless games of cowboys and Indians or whatever else young kids pretend to be. That has always been so illogical to me. I have now found that I occasionally meet someone who has the same interests as me. This is a fairly new experience and it's nice to have someone to talk to and spend time with. Don't get me wrong, I have always been a loner and don't mind at all that I am on my own, but it is nice to have a friend too. If you do have one, then try hard to keep them. I have spent years never talking to anyone at school and never wanting to, but now to have a friend is quite fun. For me, though this has given a new problem - do I tell them that I have AS? I don't want anyone to make judgements about me or treat me as if I have a disease as soon as they meet me and kids are also not really that interested in boring facts and details (apart from AS kids of course!).

My advice would be to wait and see if they say 'you are weird' – in a nice way of course if they are your friends. If they ask why you do something a bit different to others or act differently, maybe then you can just say that you think a bit differently to other people and have problems with crowds and games and loud noises or whatever. I say that my brain is slightly different and it means that I am really good at some things and not so good at others. If they are your friends they will just accept this and not make a big deal of it if you don't. Kids don't normally make as big a deal of this kind of stuff as adults do. Their parents may wonder if AS is catching – it's not by the way! All you can do is be yourself and don't bring up AS in every conversation. It may be a big deal in your life, but most kids don't understand. For older people then I would think that a good friend would be very interested in your difficulties and try to help you overcome them.

I think Mum says things to people whom she thinks will be supportive and that is really helpful. Some adults are really embarrassed to talk about things like this. Isn't that strange?! I would never be able to work out who is embarrassed and who isn't and usually get that wrong – but hey, that is their problem. I don't want to upset people unnecessarily though. That is not accepting them as they are. These things work both ways. If you want people to accept you as you are, then do the same for them, even if their ways seem weird.

For AS people, especially kids, this is all really difficult stuff to understand. I don't want to sound patronizing here. I just mean that it is virtually impossible to work out who is quite open about talking about stuff like this and who is not. I have found that sometimes people look down at the floor or away from me when I start to say something about AS. Sometimes their faces go slightly red too and sometimes they change the subject and start to talk about something else immediately. I take my cue from that and don't labour the point if I see that. Sometimes of course they may do those things and they mean something different. A red face often means that someone is merely too hot.

Parents or support workers of AS kids, please help your kids by taking away the responsibility of having to work out all this 'who to tell' stuff. They will have enough of that when they are older.

4

Fascinations and Fixations

Specialist subjects

Most people with AS have an 'obsession' or a favourite topic, or specialist subject as I prefer to call it. It is seen as one of the characteristics. These range from person to person and I am sure that some people may not even have one in particular. Surely we can't all be the same?

Although I am sure there are quite a few AS people with interests that are considered strange and obscure, I am also sure that the bulk of us do actually have interests that are pretty ordinary. In fact it is *very* unfair of the media to portray us all as people who talk continually about train timetables or constantly talk about dates and facts, or computers (although that *is* what I talk about!). We are called freaks and nerds enough anyway!

After talking to my Mum and brothers and sisters about this, it seems that the difference between someone with AS who has a fascination and someone without AS is the level of intensity of their fascination. I can only speak for myself when I say that if one subject is on my mind or I am fascinated by something, then literally everything else is insignificant. I suppose this can be seen as selfishness and I do try to think of others; sometimes it is very hard. If I am focused on my fascination, whether it is dinosaurs (when I was little I hasten to add), Pokémon, a particular PlayStation game, computers – this has always been an everlasting obsession for me – or anything else, I feel an overwhelming excitement in me that I cannot describe. I just *have* to talk about it and the irritation at being stopped can easily develop into raging fury. Now I have written that down, I can see how silly it looks and sounds, but that is just the way it is.

Sometimes, well most of the time, my mind is so full of computers that I don't stop to think about myself or other people at all. Obsessions – and I use that word for a reason – sometimes seem to creep up on me like a thief in the night. One minute I am just very interested in a topic and the next it seems as if my mind has been infiltrated by an army which stamps around and eradicates my everyday thoughts, replacing them with thoughts of computers.

It is very difficult for me to recognize that I may go on too intensely about my specialist subject as I am me and cannot imagine myself as any different. I can tell you what I am told many, many times a day. I think this is what makes my sisters say 'Luke you are such a freak' with such regularity! Apparently I talk rather too much about computers. I really do love computers, but I wouldn't call it an obsession. I suppose if anyone were to analyse me though, they would say it most certainly was as computers dominate my thoughts and my conversation.

I have my own Compaq Presario laptop computer based on Windows XP with a 56k Lucent V9.0 modem and a Pentium processor. We have broadband internet connection. That is a very high-speed connection. The girls now have a computer upstairs on their landing (though this is not connected to the internet). They also have an HP DeskJet 660 colour printer and a Snap Scan 1212 scanner. On the main computer downstairs there is an Epson Stylus C4OS and the scanner is a Packard Bell 1200. Mum bought

O

Rachel

these fairly recently because they were a 'pretty metallic blue' – written with more than a hint of scorn!

At the moment I really like finding themes for the computers off the internet. I often daydream about what backdrop I could have and what colour scheme I could use for my taskbar and message boxes. I know that I drive Mum mad with this because I keep changing things. Who says AS people don't like change? I would change the theme on my computer every few hours if it didn't cause so many arguments!

When people hear the word 'obsession' they automatically think that it is something negative or bad. That's why I prefer the term favourite topic or subject. If a fascination is channelled in the right way then it can be put to good use. For example, if computers are a person's favourite subject then they may find it easier to learn through the use of a computer rather than writing or reading books. Also, as someone grows older, they can look for jobs in that particular subject and most probably find one. Whether the fascination is trains or buildings or computers or electricity (though this is a dangerous one, I have to admit it used to fascinate me!), there is no reason at all why the child or adult cannot learn more and use their knowledge.

In some ways being so focused is a good thing. My fascination has led me to learn a lot about computers and I am definitely going to get a job in that area when I am older. I really want to program computers or make websites for professional companies. I suppose I could do both. I have a friend called Seth who has AS. He knows loads about computers. I suppose computers are his specialist subject too, but he certainly uses it well. He helps masses of people to sort out their computers. If anyone has a technical problem, then it is him that they ask. This helps other people and I am sure it makes him feel good to be needed and to be able to help. When he was at our house, he taught me a lot about the inside of a computer. It is quite strange because he is dyspraxic like me. That means that he has co-ordination problems. It seems that lots of people with AS have this to some degree or another. I have included links about that at the back. Even though Seth has these problems, he doesn't have any problem handling those tiny little parts from the inside of a computer. Seth himself told me that if you touch one contact on a circuit on the inside of a computer, it is possible to blow the whole thing – though not literally! Maybe he can do this because we have more problems with gross motor skills; that's what the bigger movements of arms and legs are called – I don't mean that the skills are gross!

I don't know about Seth or others, but I do have problems with writing and that is a fine motor skill (though if you saw my writing you would not say it was fine). This just goes to show that when someone is interested in something, then it is much easier to overcome or find ways around their difficulties.

Although it is said that people on the autistic spectrum don't like change, this cannot be entirely true as most people's obsessions and fascinations change. Maybe some last longer than others, but I think most parents and most AS or autistic kids would agree that these fascinations either get ditched in favour of a new one, or merge into something else. I now have a question for teenagers here.

Q: When is an obsession not an obsession?

A: When it is about football.

How unfair is that?! It seems that our society fully accepts the fact that a lot of men and boys 'eat, sleep and breathe' football and people seem to think that if someone doesn't, then they are not fully male. Stupid!

Girls are lucky enough to escape this football mania but I have noticed that teenage girls have to know almost every word of every song in the charts and who sang what and who is the fittest guy going, so I suppose an AS girl (or a non-AS one) that had interests other than that is likely to experience the same difficulties as a non-football crazy boy. I think an unco-ordinated AS girl is likely to have difficulties with all these dance routines that teenagers seem to do. My sisters spend hours working out amazingly complex routines and when I watch them I am almost glad to be a boy. No way could I do that and nor would I want to! AS girls, there is a light of the end of the tunnel though, because when you get to the age of fifteen or sixteen and older, these complex routines seem to be replaced by gyrating your hips and trying to look as sexy as possible. Now isn't that something to look forward to?!

I am sure that if a parent went to a doctor and said that their teenage son wouldn't shut up about football, they would laugh and tell them that it was perfectly normal. It seems as if we all have to be the same. Why can no one see that the world just isn't like that? I would like everyone to talk about computers all day actually, but I don't expect them to and people soon tell me to shut up.

Games console and computer games

Now this certainly wouldn't seem as if it was a specialist subject to most people, especially adults, but for many of us it most definitely is. It is quite strange to see that lots of AS kids and teenagers all seem to have the same kind of fascinations. Just as little autistic kids seem to be madly into *Thomas the Tank Engine*, older AS kids seem to be fascinated by Pokémon, war hammer games and figures, PlayStation and Nintendo games and computers in general. I am not saying that this is particular to AS kids, just that often we tend to get a bit carried away and take things too far (in other people's eyes).

Mum says that something becomes an addiction or an obsession when it takes an unreasonable place in your life. If something dominates your thoughts and behaviours to such an extent that the rest of your life is being interfered with, then that is the time to find ways to modify your behaviour and try 'wean yourself off it'. To be honest, I am like this with the PlayStation. Is there anyone else reading this that gets into trouble for being on the PlayStation or a games console all the time? I know that Mum will want to know the answer to why I am like this. It drives her mad. So, Mum, this one is for you! I like the PlayStation because, unlike televisions where you sit and observe other people's lives for no apparent reason and there are always repeats of the exact same thing, on a PlayStation the player actually controls the characters and there are lots of different ways to do things. Life often seems so out of control, probably for most people, so it is good to retreat into a part of life that you can control.

A television is like an extension of real life and real life is actually very difficult to work out sometimes. There are still people interacting with other people, facial expressions to work out, hidden meanings and plots to decipher. Not exactly something I want to spend my leisure time doing – I have enough of that the rest of the day! On the PlayStation the player needs to use their logic and powers of reasoning to work out a course of action to get to the next level. It is all very predictable, but not so predictable that it gets boring.

The arguments over the PlayStation are ongoing in our house. When I am on it I forget to eat, get dressed or do anything other than work out where my character is going or what it is supposed to be doing next. Mum fails to see the fascination in this and her co-ordination and concentration are very bad so she can never stop to find out how fascinating it is. There is a lot of timing and co-ordination involved in playing. Mum is perhaps *too* logical to understand these kinds of games. She says that there is no way that an animal such as 'Taz' or Bugs Bunny would be running around trying to splatter boxes and pick up apples. To me that is the fascination: a total escape from reality.

I have to admit that when I am playing I do get rather angry if someone messes up my game. My brothers and sisters will now be screaming that 'rather angry' sounds far too mild. OK, I get *very* angry! That's when Mum steps in and stops me from playing. At these times I am happy to watch one of the others play. Even though it is frustrating when the solution to a problem that someone else is trying to solve is right in front of their face but they still can't see it, I am happy to watch. It is a bit like reading. When I am reading, I have these pictures that form in my mind – it is my own little world.

Watching the PlayStation is very similar, except that this world is on the screen in front of you. Despite what Mum says, I do have fun at it even though it doesn't show on my face. My face never does seem to do the right thing! When I am watching it, it is also good to see the different solutions to problems that you cannot actually see when you are playing yourself.

Collections

Many AS people, if not all, become very attached to certain things. That's what I mean by a collection. Lots of us like to have sets of things that we can organize and categorize and line up. My Grandad collects all sorts of things and I don't think he has AS. It's not only an AS thing, I just think that it means something slightly different for AS people. In general I would say that collecting something is a pretty harmless way of feeling secure and no one should stop anyone from doing this. Organizing something is a wonderful way of shaking off the feeling of chaos that comes from living in such a disorganized world.

Again, I have had to ask my sisters and brothers and my Mum where I differ from other kids when it comes to some of my behaviours and fixations. I am actually learning about myself whilst I am writing! I sincerely hope that I am helping AS people, their parents and carers learn about AS too.

It seems that a fixation and a compulsion are different to a specialist subject and the more I think about it, the more I can see why. Mum says that though I am very annoying (gee, thanks Mum!) as I go on too much, she is glad that I have a subject that interests me so much. I am not sure that my brothers and sisters agree! Mum reckons that most parents are probably quite glad that their AS kid has a special interest as there is a good chance of them putting it to use in later life.

Sometimes, as I have said, an intense fascination for something is a good thing, but when something stops anyone being able to do other things or gets in the way of their life, then it does need to be sorted out and made to take a lower priority in their life, although I don't think one person has the right to try to completely eradicate someone else's 'obsession'. Who has the right to do that after all?

I really do want all of you parents and carers to know what your child may be thinking and feeling, rather than just snatching the thing off him or her and getting annoyed, or preventing them from performing a comforting ritual just because it is irritating. I also know from experience of talking to other AS kids that their fascinations are very much like mine so I am now going to tell you about a few things that I (and Ben and Joe too) have been attached to and the reasons for this. As you can see, some have changed as I have got older and some haven't.

Pencils

Over the years I have had many 'little idiosyncrasies', as my Granny puts it. Amongst other things, in my case (and I don't mean my pencil case – excuse the pun!), it was pencils. I think most people who remember me when I was younger, remember my pencil too. We were inseparable. I used to take pencils everywhere with me, even when we were going out. I never went anywhere without at least one pencil with me.

Rachel

I remember all this well, and the feeling of insecurity when I was without one. I suppose it was the equivalent of Ben's or Joe's dummy, though I never did suck the pencils. In fact I tapped them on everything. I think that annoyed people but I found it very relaxing and soothing. So many things in life are stressful and knowing that I had something familiar with me at all times was so, so comforting. In fact I am sighing wistfully and getting quite nostalgic at the thought! Oh well – better to have loved and lost…

At about four in the morning (I am always awake by then), Mum used to see me sliding a pencil up and down behind the door, and I always used to hear an ever weary, 'Go to bed, Luke'. At school the only problem with my love of pencils was that the school was rapidly running out of supplies. Mum used to have to buy boxes of them and take them in because I kept bringing them home. I have to say that sometimes Mum got annoyed and angry about my constant tapping and snatched my pencils off me. She even snapped one or two in half in a temper when I was tapping around in the middle of the night. She has told me that she then felt terribly guilty afterwards. You are forgiven Mum – all I did was get another pencil!

Strings and things

Another thing that I loved to do, still do actually, is to tie string everywhere. I like the idea of chain reactions – one thing happening which triggers off another, which triggers off another and so on and so on. I used to put string round a dozen objects and watch them all fall down at once. That's why I love slinkies [coiled springs] so much. When you wind one round loads of things and then let go, it pulls itself through all of them.

I suppose the rest of my family find it a bit annoying to wake up and find that their shoelaces had disappeared and were tied around their door handles! It's a bit hard to explain how rewarding and satisfying it is to tie things together. It is just one of those hypnotic things that distract me from the real world for a while and is so much fun. I wonder if my brother Matthew went out without his laces on this particular day?!

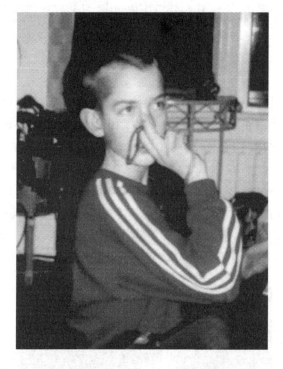

In my mind are colours and shapes and images, all distorting and merging together. I reckon that autistic kids who seem as if they are in a bubble are like this permanently. I know quite a few and wonder if their inner world is where mine used to be. Nowadays I concentrate on focusing on this world, but messing with string or luminous stuff and kaleidoscopes and lava lamps is a wonderful compromise. In this world but not of it!

Lots of kids like to unwind balls of string. It is seemingly endless and all sorts of patterns can be made whilst wrapping it around furniture. A word of warning though: don't leave a little kid with a ball of string – they may wrap it around their necks. Joe once wrapped some cotton around his toe and he had to go to the hospital to get it removed (the cotton not the toe!) as his toe had turned blue and swollen up so much. It was like a fat, little blue sausage. If you are going to let your kids have fun and get them some string to play with, then I would suggest you remove any breakables.

Batteries

If you look at any photograph of me when I was younger, then I will be holding a battery. This particular picture looked as if I was trying to pick my nose with it. It was an AA2 Duracell® unrechargeable volt battery and of course wouldn't have fitted up my nose anyway! I would have been rolling it around my face. Batteries are very good to hold. They are cool and smooth and fit perfectly in your hand – well at least the right sized ones do. I can't imagine trying to roll a 12-volt battery around my face!

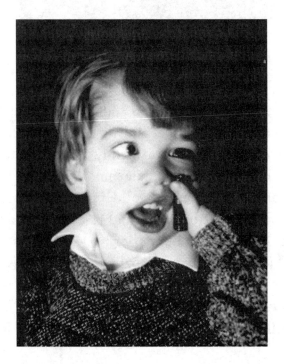

The feel of the battery is not the only reason why I used to take them out of things though. I think people presumed that I wouldn't know what they did and how they made toys and other things be activated - well I did. It is like carrying about a piece of power. I am also pretty sure that Ben and Joe think this too. We often hear the whirring of an old toy late at night as Joe has managed to put to good use one of his trusty little friends! Both of them take batteries out of everything and Ben carries them around like his prize possessions. He can't put them into things himself yet but he often brings a toy computer to us and hands us his recently acquired batteries. Joe has loads hidden in his drawers (not his pants) and under his pillows. I am not commenting on myself of course (uh hum – I have not quite grown out of this yet!). Although obsessions do wear off, I think that there is always a lasting effect after it has gone.

Another reason why I liked to collect batteries was purely and simply that I liked collecting. In a disorderly world is there anything more satisfying than organizing your possessions? I think this is why people line things up. Parents of AS or autistic kids, do you have a kid that takes the batteries out of *every* remote control? I bet lots of you do. AS kids, isn't it annoying to know that somewhere in the house there are one or two remaining?! I can sit there with my secret collection of batteries and just cannot resist the compulsion to complete the set. Uh hum…I have just realized that I have slipped into the present tense when talking about batteries. Of course I am now a cool teenager so such things really are beneath me now…*not!!*

Compulsions

Compulsions are very different to specialist subjects because they are controlling so are actually very destructive. People's compulsions can have different levels of severity. There is something called obsessive compulsive disorder, but I know very little about that apart from the name which seems quite self-explanatory. There will be information in the links at the back.

A lot of people set themselves little tasks which they find hard to break. Has anyone had to run downstairs before the toilet flush stopped? Mind you, moving house stopped that one because we are now in a bungalow! Mum says that when I was little I had to perform so many rituals before I went to bed. Now she saw these as a routine but I remember this and that wasn't quite true. Uh hum…a bit embarrassing but I actually had to kiss each wall, flick the light on and off three times, throw a particular toy out of the room and line a couple up. Now even though I was only three or four, this was a compulsion. I just *had* to do it! I cannot begin to explain the feeling if something wasn't performed. This was when I felt like my whole body was going to burst. Any of you AS people know what I mean? The urge is just *too* overwhelming.

This isn't a major problem of mine at all and if something starts to feel as if I just have to do it at any cost, then I give myself a stern talking to and negotiate my way round it. It is better to be aware of your own tendencies towards this kind of thing and then you can stop them. AS people, am I making sense? I hope so. I am merely saying that, hard as it is, it is good to be aware of yourself, your mind and your body and make sure that it does not get out of control. People can help you with this. I know it is not easy!

Controlling a compulsion

I have deliberately given this section this title because I need to tell all parents, teachers and carers to be aware that it is the compulsion that needs controlling and not the child. I don't want to appear rude, but sometimes I think that a parent may want to stop a fascination or a fixation because it is bugging them. As I have said, these are not the same as compulsions, which can take over someone's life. They are ways of feeling in control and ways of relieving stress. There is also one fact that many people seem to overlook – we actually dearly love the things we talk about. It is not just a weird quirk of AS.

For any of you that have AS or are autistic, then yes, it is up to you to control yourself, including the intensity of your fascination if it is causing a problem. I know how difficult this is and you may need help. Believe me I know! Parents and teachers, this is *not* your place! A parent or teacher should channel the fixation in another direction if it is *really* clear that the fixation is dangerous to the child or to others, or is clearly going to affect their life in a bad way. If it is not, then leave well alone and wait til they get older. Life is so controlling for us AS kids. We have to work out our ways to cope, so if spinning wheels, collecting batteries, talking about computers or whatever else on offer is a stress reliever, then my advice would be to get more batteries and leave them to it!

Having a pencil in my hand did cause me problems as I always had one hand that couldn't be used as it was occupied. This led Mum and school to help me spend some time without one. For this Mum gave me a series of charts. We started off by going without a pencil when there was a time when I wasn't stressed and had something to occupy me. This started off as a very short time, but gradually it was built up to longer periods. These times were marked down with stars and I was given a treat when I had had a good week. I remember quite clearly being given a Dennis the Menace comic. I was very proud and pleased with myself. At first, a good week was when I just had an odd star here and there, but it soon increased and I practised going without a pencil in more stressful situations. I only use pencils to write and draw with now, so whatever we did must have worked! These kinds of strategies are useful for smaller kids if there is a real problem.

Ben is the kind of child who attaches himself to things too. When he was learning to use PECS, a picture exchange system (more links at the back as usual!), the first picture Mum and Julie, his portage worker, drew was his Chinese cookery book. That was what got him used to swapping pictures for the actual item. The system worked really well for Ben and stopped him being so frustrated and angry at not being able to say what he wanted. He still uses PECS to make choices and when he is stressed and upset.

There are also 'social stories' which are pictures that help people to work through what they are feeling and help them understand things. I have to say, teenagers, that these are helpful, even at our age. It's a bit like reading a comic. Sometimes it's easier to take in. There is a link to these at the back.

Ben has a Lilliput Lane house (an ornament), a carriage clock, a soup ladle and a little box with blue beads on too. He also has a 'circle yellow dummy' – it cannot be oval, it cannot be red; no, it has to be a circle and yellow. Boy, does he scream and shout if we can't find a circle yellow dummy! The number of times we have all been running around in the evening, trying to find one whilst Ben throws a complete wobbly.

These things may not seem to be a problem but he is very little and if he carried this lot then his hands and mouth would be totally full. Mum, the child development centre (and all of us really), have worked hard at lengthening the time that Ben has gone without these things and trying to get them off him. They now take a very low priority in his life unless he is upset (although he must still have a circle yellow dummy for bed). I think he hands his dummy over without a fight when he goes to school (and he keeps his clothes on – a major achievement!).

I hope all this encourages any parents who have children that are overly attached to things. Things can change. If any of you teenagers reading this are yawning and sighing with boredom at the fact that I am again writing about when I was younger or about my brother, then just think of this. Can you say, hand on heart, that you have never been called a freak when you do something that seems odd to other people? I am sure that I am not the only one who is told to shut up as I talk about my specialist subject. Parents of smaller kids may want to know how their child's mind works, so please bear with me.

5

Sense and Sense Abilities

All of the senses – our different sensory perception

Lots of people on the autistic spectrum have trouble with their senses. We are certainly not senseless – far from it! I think that there are full books written on this subject but I must mention this because these are probably the biggest problems in our house. I have written mostly about Ben here because this is his big problem area. I know Ben is autistic, but I am sure there are kids all over the autistic spectrum who have these problems so I thought I would highlight them. I haven't asked Ben's permission to write about him because he doesn't understand, but I think he would want to help others if he could. If you can read one day, Ben, then thanks!!

AS teenagers, you may find this chapter boring, but there will be many parents and professionals who want to know about their kid, so it just has to be done. Anyway, if you read this you may recognize things in yourself from when you were younger.

Ben has sensory integrative dysfunction or tactile defensiveness or whatever else anyone likes to call this. I have read through his assessments so that I can see what words are used to describe this problem. On his statement it says that he has 'extreme difficulty with sensory stimuli'.

Touch

Ben used to have a lot more problems with textures and touch than he does now. The child development centre has worked with him at this since he was very tiny and it has really helped. At one time he used to heave and act as if he were going to throw up when he even saw paint, but now he will put up with someone painting his hand as long as it is washed immediately afterwards. He still can't stand play dough but in some ways that is a good thing because most places use wheat flour and he is on a gluten- and casein-free diet. His school makes the play dough up with rice flour so he can have a try. I think that's pretty good of them.

Ben has real problems with clothes. He will now wear them to go out to school and other places, but as soon as he comes home he strips the lot off. If he is stressed when he is out then he strips wherever he is. He is so difficult about clothes that Mum has to take him to choose his own clothes. He sits in his buggy and Mum holds the new clothes against his face or hands and he either screams 'No, hurts' or grabs it. If by some slim chance he will tolerate trying it on, then we are on a winner!

If you are a parent or work with someone like this, then don't think they are just being awkward. Things really do hurt Ben. Now he is talking better, he shouts 'Ow, hurt' at the most bizarre of things. One thing that helps if he is refusing to be dressed at all is to put a thin, long-sleeved sweatshirt on inside out and then he will put up with wearing another jumper the right way around on top. If it is really cold and Mum is trying to get him to wear something at home, he will sometimes wear a T-shirt inside out. This doesn't help with the trousers and shoes, but it's a start!

Ben had a little friend called Emma and she hated her clothes on too. If she spilled even a drop of something on her clothes then she pulled them off immediately. That is another thing for a parent of an autistic child to think about if the child keeps taking his or her clothes off. Emma was very particular about having things just as she wanted; a place for everything and everything in its place. Funnily enough she had the opposite problems with sound to Ben. For Emma, loud was best. She banged on her drum whilst Ben cringed with his fingers in his ears. They do say opposites attract!

Sand is another thing that Ben used to hate. Me and Mum are exactly the same. Mum has all these sensory problems and more besides. Ben will now play with dry sand, though not wet. I still hate being sticky and slimy but I too can tolerate warm, dry sand once I take a deep breath and go for it. Still not my idea of fun though! I will now tell you a story that illustrates how much trouble these sensory problems can cause, in the hope that you may recognize some behaviours of your child and learn a bit more about them. If not it will make you laugh!

A Tiptoe Down Memory Lane

Are you sitting comfortably? Then I will begin! (My Grandad always says that, apparently it comes from a very old children's radio programme.)

One day we decided to go out. It was a boiling hot day so Mum had decided that we should go to St Anne's beach. I hated beaches and sand and sun and water, even more than I do now, so it just was not my idea of a good time! As usual though, the majority ruled and off we went (even though I think all will agree that I put up a good fight).

When we got there, Mum carried me down across the sandhills on her back so that I didn't have to get my feet sandy or wet and settled me down on a towel – still moaning I hasten to add! My sisters were as usual, very scornful and bad tempered about the fact that I hated this so much. In my opinion they are the freaks for liking this kind of stuff.

Once on the beach, my sisters soon ran off to get muddy and sticky and wet (and they say I am weird!) and left me sitting on a towel working out bits of mental arithmetic to keep myself occupied. Mum was busy with Joe who was only about four and very little but she interspersed this with the occasional 'Go and play with your sisters, Luke' or 'Just give it a go, you may like it'. I sat and thought 'Yeah, about as much as reclining in a vat full of acid', but eventually I dutifully got up and wandered in the direction of my sisters, trying to tiptoe to avoid as much of the sand as possible, whilst casting mournful faces at a smiling, applauding Mum.

As I walked and tolerated the disgusting feeling of wet sand between my toes, the attraction of the warm grass and the reed-type plants sticking out of the grass was too much for me and I turned and wandered to a particular big patch of grass, never giving anyone else a second thought.

One second I was there, the next, poof – I was gone, or so it seemed to them. In actual fact, I was picking all the little seeds off this piece of grass and then trying to fold it and blow between it. Have you ever tried that? Be careful though, because grass is like paper and can cut you. If you get it right, it makes a really cool squealing noise. I never can quite manage it.

I often get engrossed in one thing or another and lose track of time. I think it's a pity that time exists at all, but then I suppose at least we know when to have meals. I can spend hours looking at the patterns and shapes in things around me. I carry in my head my own little show of patterns and prisms and shapes and colours. They intermingle with shapes from the outside world. It is very hard to explain, but maybe other AS or autistic people understand. Strangely enough, as I get older I am more aware of time and space and people and less aware of my own little world. I think when I used to 'get lost' (I have put that in inverted commas because I only got lost in other people's eyes, I always knew where I was), I was in my own world quite a lot. Ben is like that now.

After a while, I decided to go back to Mum. I was told that it was a very long while, many hours actually, but I didn't realize that. One small problem with going back to Mum was that I didn't particularly know which way back was. I looked round for a while and finally saw a man walking along in the grass. He asked if I was lost. I explained that I wasn't lost but I didn't know where my Mum was and had he seen her. I explained that she had curly hair and pink lipstick and the last time I saw her she was sat on a pyramid. Looking back on it now, I suppose he was very puzzled. We were in St Anne's, not Egypt! The pyramid is a big, sloping stone wall with two faces, which look like that of a pyramid. It did to me anyway, but apparently not to others!

Meanwhile, Mum had got every single person on the beach looking for me. Coastguards, police, a pack of Brownies and every available person were all shouting my name over a loudspeaker. I didn't hear a thing! I have a strange kind of hearing and can only concentrate on listening to things if I know I am meant to. Distinguishing between background and foreground noise has always been a problem, so however loud they shouted I would have presumed that it was background noise. This is a difficulty of AS because I get told off so many times for being an ignorant pig when I genuinely do not recognize that I am being spoken to. Joe has this problem a lot, lot worse than I do.

I wasn't really looking for anyone when I was found. I just stumbled across them. It was very

strange because my sisters and brothers were crying
and Mum grabbed me and a big fuss was made over
what seemed to me like nothing. Sometimes it is
very hard to understand exactly what I have done
wrong. If you are a parent and your child is like
that, then make sure you explain to them very
clearly.

PRESSURE

A lot of AS and autistic people try to find things to help them to
feel secure or even to block out the world. When I was younger,
my balaclava was something that gave me great security. I used to
wear it twenty-four hours a day, seven days a week. I wore it in
classes at school, at mealtimes, everywhere. I don't think most of
my friends at school had actually seen my face! I wonder if it ever
got washed?

The reason I liked my balaclava so much was because it was
more than just a comfort. It served a purpose. The first thing it did
was to shield my ears from some of the noise that went on all day,
every day. I have very sensitive hearing and this is such a noisy
world. The balaclava muffled that slightly and changed the way
things sounded. That wasn't the main reason for it, though; it was
just an added bonus. The main reason was that I felt safe behind it.
It was as if I was somehow watching this confusing world from
behind a secure screen and the pressure and tightness of the
material around my head and face was like being squeezed constantly. Ben wears a pair of earmuffs, a pair of goggles, or both, for
a lot of the time. He won't sleep without them. I presume this is for
the same reasons. He looks very cute now, as you can see from the

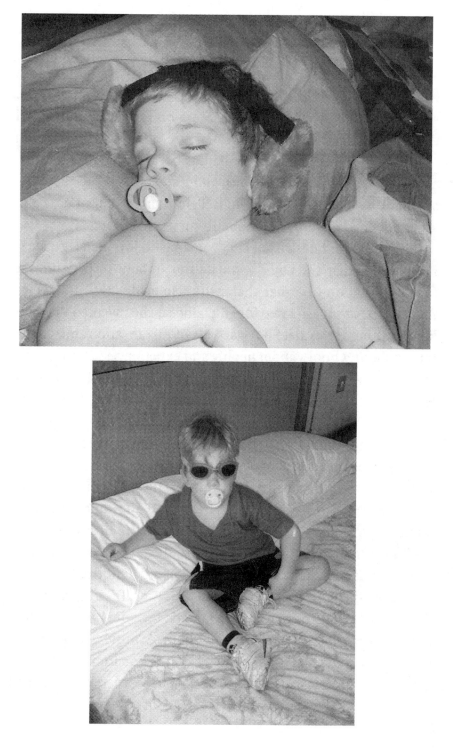

photograph, but I bet he would get teased if he carried on as he gets older!

Ben often wants us to stick our fingers very hard into his eyes (we don't do it hard of course) and squeeze his feet very tightly. He will only sleep with someone squeezing his feet, at the moment. I think that is because he likes the pressure, a bit like my balaclava experience. Ben is also very dangerous because he 'ducks under'. Ben ducks under tables, cushions, quilts and clothes. He climbs up anyone's jumpers and buries himself in them. Mum often walks around like a kangaroo with him in the pouch!

Temple Grandin is an autistic woman who invented a 'squeeze machine' so that she could regulate the amount of pressure she felt. She went on to realize that cattle also made more milk when they had been squashed up together and so she invented the same kind of thing for cattle. She has loads of qualifications in agriculture and writes books about her life and experiences. This just goes to show how someone who is different can have a very productive and good life. Again, I have put links about this at the back. (Sorry, I am beginning to act like a stuck record!)

My balaclava was phased out gradually by my being allowed to have some times with my balaclava on and getting a reward if I would put up with some time without. This was difficult at first but I got some cool books and treats and the time without it increased so much that it became unnecessary. If any parent is reading this and trying to get their child to let go of something that really is inappropriate (not just what a parent thinks is inappropriate), then the tip here is to take your time. Pick times that are the least stressful and reward them loads for going without for a tiny bit; then increase the time without. We did star charts to record how well I had done. Star charts are good for people on the autistic spectrum because things are so much easier to understand when they can be seen. At the moment Ben would pick the stars off and eat them, but I am sure they will help him one day.

Vision

I think that a lot of AS or autistic people have different perception rather than their actual vision being different. I know this from looking at Ben. When we are out and there are lines painted on the floor, he drops down to his knees to crawl over them, but the eye clinics insist he can see better than that. I think things must get distorted and muddle him up. I think a lot of this is to do with his balance. He hates swings or being high up. Apparently all of this is something to do with sensory dysfunction and I am putting links at the back so that you can find out more.

Another problem people have is being able to see things out of 'the corner of their eye'. Mum can spot something moving slightly in the corner of the room and this drives her absolutely mad. No one is allowed to even move their fingers, never mind tap them when she is around. I reckon that this is a handy thing to have if you want to check out some fit girl without appearing too obvious!

I don't have any of these problems apart from the fact that I don't see very well out of my left eye and have needed loads of operations to stop me being cross-eyed. I also have this nystagmus (wobbly eyes). I do have a problem pulling my eyes away from all glittery, shiny things. I have always liked lights and have loads in my room. I have a lava lamp, a disco ball, a UFO lamp and a magic mushroom (this is what I call my spherical lamp with lights on before any of you who know about drugs get worried!). They are just hypnotic and soothing and such a wonderful escape from reality. In a lot of special schools they have 'sensory rooms' with loads of different lights and sounds in them. My idea of heaven!

EYE CONTACT

'Are you listening to me?' 'Look at me when I am talking to you.' AS kids, how familiar are those words? Don't they just make you groan? (And that's putting it politely!) Adults seem to make a really big deal of getting people to look at them when they are talking. Apparently it is seen as rude if you don't look at least in the direction of the speaker. This world is full of so many stupid rules! I really hate this one.

Joseph rarely looks at anyone when they are talking to him and part of the work they do at school is to get him to do so. I can see the reason why they do this with Joe because he has a big listening and attention problem. When he is not looking at someone he is usually doing his own thing and people are wasting their time talking to him. To find out whether your child or the person you are working with or talking to is listening, the easiest way is to ask them a question related to what you have just said. If they answer and are obviously listening, then personally I think it is irrelevant whether they are looking at you or not.

When I look someone straight in the eye, particularly someone I am not familiar with, the feeling is so uncomfortable that I

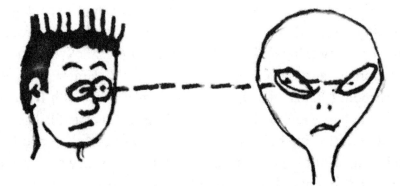

Sarah

cannot really describe it. First of all I feel as if their eyes are burning me and I really feel as if I am looking into the face of an alien. I know this sounds rude but I am telling it how it is. If I get past that stage and don't look away, then whilst someone is talking I find myself staring really hard and looking at their features and completely forgetting to listen to what they are saying. Mum says when I was little I used to go right up to people and stare in their faces. They probably looked funny – I often have to stop myself from giggling when I examine people's faces; there are some very strange ones around!

Sometimes it is too hard to concentrate on listening and looking at the same time. People are hard enough to understand as their words are often so very cryptic, but when their faces are moving around, their eyebrows rising and falling and their eyes getting wider then squinting, I cannot fathom all that out in one go, so to be honest I don't even try.

AS kids, I have found a compromise to this problem that I am practising and working well on. I look at people's mouths. That means that the other person is satisfied enough because you are looking in their direction but yet you do not have to have that horrendous, burning into your very soul feeling that comes with staring into someone's eyes. Just try looking hard at someone's mouth when they are talking and see how many shapes it makes. The trouble with this is the temptation to amuse yourself with this and forget to listen. Another good ploy is to look in the direction of the speaker's ear. This is a good one because it reminds you to listen and provides no distractions (unless of course you find someone with a wiggly one!).

It is best to find some kind of compromise so that you don't stand out too much and appear rude. It can be done. Remember, there is more than one way to skin a cat! (Mum told me this one – I think it sounds horrible.)

SPINNING

I know this is not exactly to do with vision but, as I have said, I think that autistic people's balance and perception are often different. (I also couldn't work out where else to put this section!) Spinning seems to be something to do with this imbalance.

Right up to this day I have always loved spinning around. Honest – I am not spinning a yarn! In fact my best things are computers, lights and spinning (in that order). This is something to do with sensory input and the links at the back will help you find more information. Don't forget that I am only thirteen so I don't know everything (I do love using that excuse!).

Here's yet another little story to illustrate the part these sensory issues have played in our lives. I hope I am not boring you! AS kids, can you think of any times when these kinds of things have got you into trouble? I have found it fun to remember these things.

Up, Up and Away...

We were at Butlins and we were at an amusement park there. One minute I was with Mum and my brothers and sisters and the next I looked up and saw a ride with rockets spinning overhead. I couldn't resist and quietly squeezed between the ride operator's legs and onto a rocket.

I didn't give anyone else a second thought. I don't, when something captures my attention, but I am learning to try. It is only fair. If you have AS (or if you don't) and are reading this, then do try to do the same.

Mum turned round, saw I was gone, and then did the thing she is best at. She got every 'Tom, Dick and Harry' (isn't that a strange one?!) in the whole place looking for me. She has had a lot of practice at that! She finally found me in a state of bliss. Sitting down on the floor of the rocket. I had made myself comfortable and was quite content to spin around and around and around.

When I eventually got off (apparently it was over three hours and the police had been called!) Mum wasn't angry, just plain puzzled. How could I have stayed in the same place for so long and not realized people would be looking for me?

When I think of one thing, I think of that and only that. When I am spinning or gazing at coloured or flashing things I am oblivious to the world.

Hearing

The people who have most problems with sound nowadays are Ben and, strangely, Mum. She hates going to the cinema and things like that because they are too loud and when we do she just sits there with earplugs or her fingers in her ears, jumping a mile when there is a bang or something. Mum has what some people would call bionic ears. When she is in her bedroom she can hear someone whispering very clearly on the other side of the house. I think it is amazing, but Mum just thinks it is annoying.

Ben cannot manage to go to the cinema because there are too many onslaughts to his sensory problems in one go. We tried once and he dropped to the floor with his hands over his ears and his eyes squeezed shut, screaming 'too noisy' and 'not dark'. We had to take him home. Ben spends a lot of time with his fingers in his ears, but he is much better if we tell him exactly what is going to happen.

Sarah

We can now tell him we are going to vacuum and then he scuttles off into another room with his fingers in his ears and slams the door behind him. (He does that anyway, he has a thing about slamming doors.) I used to have the same sound problems but they have eased off. The only thing I cannot stand is the echoing in swimming baths or big empty halls. There is another thing that I find really annoying and that is the fact that exams are taken in big halls. I can hear everyone turning their pages on their exams sheets and this drives me crazy.

Taste

This is a problem for a lot of autistic people. Some people like really bland things, some like really spicy or highly flavoured things. It seems as if the taste buds are over- or underdeveloped. I like really hot and spicy things myself but I wouldn't say it was extreme. I don't think the food problems that many autistic and AS kids have are due to them disliking the taste as most won't even try new things. It is to do with the presentation, the texture and the smell of food as well as them needing sameness.

Smell

Again this is an area that used to be more of a problem to me than it is now. I know I am being a bore, but a lot of sensory issues disappeared when I went gluten and casein free. Parents of AS kids, things do get easier. I still cannot bear to go past fish shops and the smell of strong perfumes makes me sneeze, but apart from that fairly normal response this is not a problem area. Mum, however, has a nose like a bloodhound. She is always complaining of smells that other people are not aware of. Often we go into a shop and she goes pale and says how much something stinks, but no one else can smell a thing. It is also a good thing because she absolutely loves some smells. The smell of certain flowers instantly puts her in a good mood, but unfortunately my sister Sarah is allergic to them!

For those AS teenagers who are lucky enough to get a date, then I can imagine a heightened sense of smell could be a problem. Don't go saying to your date 'yuck your perfume stinks' or they will very soon become an ex! I suppose you could carefully tell them that a lot of smells irritate your nose and would they mind not wearing as much next time you see them.

All in a jumble

Ben often claps his hands over his ears when the light is suddenly turned on or off, or shuts his eyes tightly when there is a strong smell about (doesn't he Joe – snigger!). I think people on the autistic spectrum often get their senses jumbled up. Here's another little story when it seems that I did just that.

Muddled Up Senses?

Mum thought we should go out for the day, and after about an hour of squabbling it was decided that we were going to go to the zoo. There were lions, snakes, tigers, deer, monkeys, lemurs and finally the gorillas. I was looking at all the animals and I was all fine and dandy until we came to the gorillas. I took one look at them and felt that familiar feeling wash over me. I then turned and threw up right there where I was standing. It's strange how when you feel sick, if you are actually sick you always feel a lot better. I am not really sure why I was sick, I mean, they are only our unevolved ancestors.

From then on things went downhill! Every time I looked at another lot of animals – any animals – I threw up again. Mum walked pushing the buggy with Joe in with one hand and using her other hand to cover my eyes. I wasn't sick when I couldn't see the animals and as soon as I took a peek – I also took a puke!

Watching Ben put his hands over his ears when the lights are too bright makes me wonder whether it was the smell of the gorillas that set off the sickness and then all the smells became too bad to tolerate. I know I wasn't having my nose covered, but maybe I too got my senses muddled up.

6

A Different Physiology

All these problems with the senses and the fact that so, so many people have stomach and bowel problems (and there was me thinking I had got away without writing about poo in this book!) indicate to me the fact that there is something slightly different about our make-up (not lipstick and stuff!) from other people. The fact that loads of scientists throughout the world have already come to that conclusion kind of helps me to work that one out anyway! I am not that clever and after all I am only thirteen!

There seems to be no definite cause of autism and lots of people have different theories. Research is going on all around the world to find both the cause and a cure. This is a really controversial subject because lots of people (me included) think that looking for a cure for autism can be likened to Hitler trying to create an Aryan race. I am ducking for cover here because I am sure that there are loads of people reading this and screaming it is fine for me to say, but I should have their problems or see their kid before I make such statements. Personally, I think that these kinds of debates get complicated because a lot of people don't distinguish between high functioning autistic and AS people (I never have been quite sure of the difference between those two) and low functioning and very severely autistic people.

I know that we are all on the spectrum and are variations on a theme, but I can fully understand why a parent would want a 'cure' for a person who is incontinent, bangs their head all the time, bites themselves and has no form of communication.

I certainly wouldn't be cured or strip my brothers of their personalities, but I do think that it would be good to find a 'cure' for some of the really awful parts of autism such as the stomach and bowel problems, fears, compulsions and sensory problems.

In our family we have a history of allergies. My Aunty Heather has so many allergies you just wouldn't believe it. Tons of foods – eggs, fish, nuts and others, most animals, latex, dust – you name it, she is allergic to it! She has an immune problem and takes loads of drugs and steroids and allsorts to stop her body rejecting the things that she is allergic to. She has terrible asthma and eczema and hay fever and terrible stomach problems. (Sorry Aunty Heath, I make you sound a right mess!)

Joe and Ben and Anna and Mum have asthma too, though not like Aunty Heather's – hers is really bad. Sarah is allergic to a lot of animals and has really bad hay fever. Granny is diabetic and has problems with dairy stuff. Joe has inherited the food allergies mainly. He gets so ill with gluten and dairy stuff. Properly ill, not just wacky behaviours. He comes out in big red lumps and can't breathe if he touches eggs and something make his lips come up in blisters. We haven't found out what does that yet.

I can just imagine (see I can do it!) you all muttering 'So what?' or at least a polite 'Well what has that got to do with Asperger Syndrome?' The reason is because it shows that there is an immune problem throughout our family. I know that the same is true of masses of other families too. These immune problems all seem to be linked to autism. Don't ask me how. I am only a kid and am going to work with computers anyway, not be a biologist or a doctor!

Some families will have an autistic kid, or you may be autistic or AS and have none of these problems in the family. There is obviously a genetic factor involved with autism as so many families have more than one person with autism or AS or other related 'disorders'. (Don't you just hate that word? I am actually very ordered!) All the controversy surrounding vaccinations must be for a reason. There is no smoke without fire. I am not going into that subject because I haven't got a clue, but it does seem logical to me that if the immune system of some people is a bit dodgy (hardly scientific, I know, but hey…), then doses of diseases are likely to tip their body over the edge and cause all sorts of problems, especially when more than one disease is given at the same time.

Then again, some people have had vaccinations and been fine and some people have had none and are autistic. I keep saying that we are all different and I am sure there are different causes and triggers for different people. I do think that parents should be allowed to make those decisions for themselves and money should be put into researching these links properly instead of being spent on adverts designed to scare people and use emotional blackmail. I am pretty sure that there are heavy vaccination programmes in most countries, so if each government kept a record of who had been vaccinated with what (I think they do anyway), which kids had problems before vaccination anyway, listened to the parents that said their kid regressed afterwards and which kids became autistic when they were older, then surely they could see whether there was a link or not at some point. The trouble with this kind of stuff goes back to what I said in my earlier chapters. Who diagnoses? What problems are they looking for? Who keeps the records? Oops…I did say I wasn't going to go into that subject!

Vaccinations, genetics, brain problems, immune problems – I don't really know, but it does seem as if a lot of autistic people seem to have a different physiology from other people and more and more research seems to be showing this.

I don't know about any of you AS readers, but I know that I have taken drugs in my life (not illegal ones…no way! I have written about that later) and they have affected me in a different way from how they do other people.

When I was eight years old I had to have a brain scan in hospital. I used to have fits, apparently. I had to be put to sleep for the brain scan, and to put me to sleep I had to take some brown medicine. The difficult part for the nurses and Mum was to get me to take it. It was disgusting, so naturally I spat it out and vomited back the bit that did go down. They eventually held me down and, though I fought like mad, they got some into me and waited for it to take effect. Well they waited…and they waited…and they waited! It got later and later and still I was bouncing around quite happily. The whole nasty performance was repeated hours later as I was still awake. Still I didn't sleep. This time, though, I remember quite clearly that it seemed as if the floor was made of sponge – it was *so* cool! I never did get the brain scan that day.

The same kind of thing used to happen when I had operations on my eyes. When I went for my first operation I was given a pink medicine to help me get sleepy before I went – well it certainly didn't do that. It had the opposite effect! I was giggling one minute and shouting the next and then getting angry the minute after that. Mum says I was uncontrollable. On future operations, they made sure no one gave me the pink medicine. Apparently this kind of thing happens a lot with AS and autistic people so, parents, don't be surprised when your child is still bounding about after being given a sedative or that you yourself feel even more awake after taking a sleeping pill.

The reason I had operations on my eyes was because I was born with extremely wobbly and squiffy eyes. The proper name for it is

nystagmus and strabismus. I have worn patches and had operations to sort out the fact that my eyes were so turned in. The stupid
thing is now one turns out instead. They overdid the tightening of
the muscles, I think. I wonder how many of you AS kids reading
this have a 'lazy' eye or need glasses? It seems like loads of other
AS and autistic people do. Ben has the same problem now and
wears patches and glasses.

Here's a quick biology lesson. Serotonin is a hormone secreted
from the pineal gland and also in a smaller amount in the retina.
This is needed to regulate our bodies to recognize night and day. I
find it quite interesting that a lot of AS and autistic people have
nystagmus (wobbly eyes) and strabismus (squint) and also have
sleep problems, when this serotonin is produced in smaller
amounts in the retina. I know that the pineal gland is the main part
of the body that produces serotonin, but even so all this is interesting and there may be a link.

Any teenagers that are reading this and wondering if any of
this stuff applies to them, then just remember that AS is an autistic
spectrum disorder so even though we may not be affected in the
same way as someone on the lower end of the spectrum, it doesn't
mean that it doesn't apply. It's all interesting stuff.

Dietary differences

What are your favourite foods? Parents, what are your child's
favourite foods and will they only eat certain ones? Let me guess –
chicken nuggets, pizza, pasta, toast, cheese, ice cream, yoghurts,
custard creams, chocolate and milk. Well, am I right? Maybe you
are the opposite and absolutely loathe milk or never eat bread.
Sometimes people's bodies are clever and suss out for themselves
that something is causing a problem.

There is a theory that gluten and casein (the proteins found in
four grains and in dairy produce) cannot be broken down properly

Anna

in people on the autistic spectrum. Peptides are then produced which leak into the bloodstream. Gluten breaks down into a peptide called gluteomorphine and casein breaks down into a peptide called caseomorphorphine. As you can guess by the name, these have the effect of morphine and are just as addictive. These peptides whizz around the body, into the brain and cause the person to respond differently to all sorts of stimuli. By removing the offending foods (those which contain gluten and casein) from your or your child's diet, the production of these peptides stops and so the 'heroin' effect stops too. This is a very simplified version of this theory and there are other books that go into the fine detail of what this diet entails and how to do it. I will give a shameless plug here and say that one of them is mine! I wrote a full book about how the removal of gluten, casein, aspartame and monosodium glutamate changed the lives of me and my brothers and how I feel if I eat this stuff.

For all of you teenagers reading this and thinking that you would never be able to do without your pizzas or your bars of chocolate – you don't have to. There are loads of decent foods that are acceptable for the diet and in some ways having AS and being gluten and casein free (GF/CF) is probably easier than for people without AS. We are less likely to have as many social occasions where everyone is eating and we are more likely to stick to the rules of the diet. I do miss some foods and I do 'cheat' and have stuff that I shouldn't occasionally, but then I regret it.

If you were sighing as you read this and wondering how it bears any relation to teenage problems, then just think of this. How many times have you been told that you look like death warmed up? How many times have you been told that your breath stinks? How many times have you been teased about your glowing red ears? Have you ever had to rush off to the loo or try to pretend that that disgusting smell comes from someone else? Believe me – I know from experience that all these things hardly increase your chances of making friends, and particularly making friends (and hopefully more!) with the opposite sex. If eating different foods, taking enzymes, taking vitamins or anything else, helps this kind of stuff then it is surely worth a try. It has made a massive difference to my life and the lives of many others and if it doesn't help, then no harm has been done.

All around the world, scientists are investigating all the links between this kind of stuff and autism. There is the Autism Research Institute in the USA and the Autism Research Unit in Sunderland, UK, and I am sure there are many, many more. Apart from the fact that I am speaking straight from the horse's mouth (don't laugh, just look it up!), I suppose I am no expert.

I went to see Paul Shattock of the Sunderland Autism Research Unit to talk about all sorts of biological aspects of autism and I found him really interesting. (I am not just creeping here, Paul, either!) It was very scientific and he talked a lot about chains of peptides and amino acids and dopamine levels and all sorts of fairly complicated stuff, but yet I really enjoyed it. I like to learn.

There seem to be so many things that you can try to help either yourself or your child. Like I have said, there are some parts of autism and AS that are pretty awful.

Paul Shattock has written a Sunderland Protocol (have a look at the Diet website links), which gives a structured way of implementing a biological approach to dealing with autism. There are also DAN (Defeat Autism Now) doctors throughout the world who are dedicated to using different biological interventions to help people to get the best life possible. Some of these interventions are:

- removal of casein
- removal of gluten
- removal of exito toxins (aspartame and monosodium glutamate)
- allergy testing and removal of any other allergens
- treatment of candida and other yeast or parasite problems
- probiotics
- essential fatty acids
- Epsom salts (these go in the bath, you don't eat them!)
- digestive enzymes (there are more and more reports that these are making massive differences to some people)
- trace elements and minerals
- vitamin therapy
- mega doses of vitamin B6
- secretin
- homeopathic remedies.

These haven't been put in any particular order or importance, although it is generally thought that the removal of the peptides caused by gluten and casein and the removal of exito toxins are the first things to do as these can mask all sorts of other problems. (Also please take a look at the Diet website links.)

Mum works on the helplines for a charity called Allergy induced Autism (AiA). That's how she first met Marilyn Le Breton who has written a book about how to implement this diet and also the AiA GF/CF recipe book. There are also books written that are aimed at worldwide readers, though mainly America. I have included all these in the Further Reading section at the back.

Although it amazes me how many people have their kids on the diet and are treating them for candida and doing all sorts of biological stuff, I am always aware that a lot of people seem to think that this will only help small and severely autistic kids. That just isn't so. If you are a teenager reading this, then it really is worth looking up more details and seeing whether you may benefit from it. I would say go for it, but the ball really is in your court!

7

A Word about Sleep

I have written in the previous chapter how a lot if not all people on the autistic spectrum seem to be 'wired' rather differently to other people and, amongst other things, many of us have sleeping problems – or rather *not* sleeping problems! I have had enormous problems both getting to and staying asleep ever since the day I was born. It is a real pain I can tell you. You just cannot imagine what it feels like to lie there bored senseless, awaiting daylight and the time when it is deemed OK to get up. Actually, if you are AS yourself then maybe you can. A few of my most vivid memories

Anna

are of lying awake in my cot and screaming to get out. I remember clinging on to the bars and being very angry and screaming the place down. I remember quite clearly sticking my foot through the bars and being *so* annoyed that the rest of me didn't follow. I remember the colours of my curtains, the bedding and everything. I liked everything to be pink at that time. (I hasten to add that I did grow out of this!)

Many a night, in fact most nights in the past, I used to lie awake and wonder what I was meant to do. Has anyone ever noticed how slowly time seems to pass when you are lying or sitting there doing absolutely nothing? As I got older I read instead of getting angry. I used to read around two regular-sized books a night, but now I read one and wait for my eyes to start to droop and I do sleep for an odd time here and there. Some times I don't, though, and then I get shouted at for looking like 'death warmed up'.

Ben has the same problems with not being able to sleep. He is learning to talk now and it helps to understand him better. He now screams and pulls at his eyelids when they droop and says 'the eyes make him dark'. He doesn't like the dark. I didn't used to like the dark either. My room and my things are familiar, my security. The dark creeps in and steals that familiarity and security away. I don't mind it now because I know it, but I think Ben is going through the same thing.

There seems to be two kinds of sleep problems. There are the problems with getting to sleep and the problem with staying asleep. We have a mixture between us all in our family.

Medication

For me, getting to sleep has been the biggest problem because I can't stay asleep if I can't even get there in the first place. For this problem, the doctor prescribed some medicine to help us get to sleep, but Mum doesn't really like drugs unless things get really desperate so this stuff hadn't been used. One night things got really desperate!

A Story of Stupidity

I cringe at the thought of even telling this tale but I suppose it is very important for AS people and parents and carers to realize that even someone as…errmm…witty and charming and intelligent as myself can, very occasionally, do something that is very, very stupid.

Medicines in our house are kept well out of reach of Ben and Joe, but I am bigger and I presume Mum reckoned that it was OK to have the medicines in a high-up cupboard. She was right in a way. I am not stupid and wouldn't dream of taking medicines unnecessarily.

It was 1am and I was not even slightly tired. Mum had already been down at midnight and shouted at me for messing around in the games room and I knew I should go to sleep so here's what I did. I went to the medicine cabinet and took about half a bottle of this sedative. Amitryptiline it was called. I know…stupid, stupid, stupid!!

My logic was simple. I figured that as it was prescribed for Ben who was much smaller and younger than me, then I would have to take an awful lot for me to get to sleep when I wasn't even tired anyway. Duh!! I was most definitely *wrong*! When I took it, I was in hospital, unconscious on a life support machine for two or three days. My reason, though, for this was *not* suicide as I think some people may have thought. I found that extremely insulting and quite hurtful. One doctor suggested I see a psychiatrist! I think that suicide, however bad someone feels, is very selfish as other people will be upset. I also think that it would be very wrong. It is up to each one of us to sort out any problems we have and get on with the life we are given.

The main reason why I found this insulting, though, is because that automatically makes judgements about my character and my family. I was and am very happy with my life and consider myself to be very lucky. We have a very big house with a bedroom for each of us, a posh car, a massive trampoline and almost any other thing we could ever want. Most of all, though, I have a wonderful happy family (despite Sarah's moods!). We have a lot of fun together and I couldn't wish for anything else.

Mum has now spelled out to me all about drugs and things in more detail and the doctors told me how lucky I am too. I certainly won't make that mistake again. We now have a lock on the medicine cabinet with a really deafening buzzer which goes off when anyone opens it, so no one can even take a vitamin without half the street knowing! One thing I will say is that I think I gave Mum and everyone a scare, so make sure that you don't take anything at all without checking first.

If you are a parent of any child, AS or not, then I would say, just have medicines locked away. I am not being arrogant (my sisters will now laugh scornfully at that) but I think I am quite intelligent and yet I am still pretty embarrassed at doing something so daft. Thank you to everyone who looked after me and sorry for being such an idiot. Thank you too to Dr Stevens for realizing that I made a mistake (rather an understatement), rather than thinking I was suicidal!

Medication can work for some people, however. Personally I think it is better to do without drugs if at all possible and I am sure most other people do too, but sometimes it is not possible. I cannot write about what drugs work and don't because I am thirteen (or have I not told you yet?) and it is not my place to do so. All I can do is emphasize what I said in Chapter 6 – that a lot of people on the autistic spectrum don't seem to respond to drugs in the same way as others.

A lot of people use melatonin to help their child or themselves get to sleep. It is available in America and other countries fairly freely I think. Most doctors don't give it anyone here, although I believe a few do. It is meant to be safe and work for a lot of people. We can't get it unfortunately.

If things are really bad, though, go to the doctor and talk about it. Any doctors reading this – please don't underestimate the extent of this problem. I cannot begin to describe how awful it is to know that sleep is needed but not be able to do it. People don't want to drug their kids and I don't think that people themselves want to be drugged, so if they come to you, they are at the end of their rope. Try to help them please. Thanks!

Sleeping solutions for people with AS

I am sure that lots of you have the same problem with sleep, so I will write here a load of tips that I have been given over the years in the hope that some may help some of you. Different things work for different people. Different strokes for different folks!

I have actually tried every method everyone told me. Some have been known to work with other people, some were strange, some seem just plain stupid, but I will write them anyway. See what you think and good luck.

1. When you go to bed at night, try imagining a bicycle and zoom in to a small detail on the bike, such as the spokes. Apparently, if you hold that in your mind then you eventually go to sleep. Now in my opinion, this is one of the ones that is just plain stupid! AS people have no difficulty whatsoever in focusing on small details, in fact we have difficulty seeing the whole picture and tend to only focus on small details. I thought it was worth mentioning just in case, by some strange chance, it worked for someone reading this. It certainly didn't for me!

2. Another one of these kinds of ideas is to imagine a black sheet of rippling black velvet. Again that is meant to put you to sleep. Not me, it makes me cringe – I hate the feel of velvet!

3. If you know that you only need three, four or five hours of sleep and you genuinely do feel fine in the day, then don't let it bother you that others sleep for longer. We are the lucky ones because we can get more done. Just remember to be quiet and don't do anything dangerous whilst others are sleeping.

4.   One thing that is necessary I reckon and has made a difference to our family is blackout curtains. This all supports the lack of serotonin theory that I mentioned earlier.

5.   Something like the computer on standby can be enough to keep you awake (thanks for that Seth!). Check your room carefully and make sure no sounds or smells are bugging you.

6.   Although we have to make sure that we are not so bound up by routines that it ruins our lives, a familiar routine in the evening can help you to settle. I have my own little routines now which I perform each night.

7.   A step-by-step list of what to do once in the bedroom can help immensely. To have a very clear idea of what you are meant to be doing is very comforting and there is no need to let anyone know you have this if you feel silly.

8.   Make sure that your school bag is packed, school uniform is ready and your homework is done (or at least that your excuse is well planned!). If you are an adult, make sure your work stuff is prepared.

9.   Some people (my Mum being one) have difficulty with their minds working so fast that they can't settle. Going to bed with headphones playing your favourite music can help this. It helps clear your mind.

10.   If you have lots of negative stuff on your mind, then it's a good idea to write it down and then throw the paper away. I know there are those of us who are so logical and literal that we cannot see this as actually throwing

away our negative thoughts, after all it's only a piece of paper, but I have heard that it works for some.

11. I would say here that if you are just writing angry (or other...!) feelings down, then you can be as graphic as you like. Now is the time to get it all out of your system! If you are thinking swear words and being upset, then now is your time to write all the stuff that you are not allowed to say. Remember to throw it away properly afterwards. This can be therapeutic as long as you realize that this should be the *only* time you do stuff like this.

12. If it is stuff that needs doing that is bothering you, then make yourself a concise list for the day after. When all this is done, you can then go through your bedtime routine of getting into bed, etc. again.

13. Although I have a sneezy sister and a Mum with a nose like a bloodhound (that means she can smell things too acutely) so smelly alternatives are not so viable here, aromatherapy seems to help many people. An oil burner put somewhere safe with a relaxing smell such as lavender is very calming.

14. A warm bath with oils or scents in may help, though I have to say that the idea of putting something in the bath to help an AS kid sleep seems a massive contradiction in terms. How many of you like bathing? I don't!

15. Health shops sell a variety of remedies that are supposed to help with sleep problems. Bach flower and valerian are a couple we have tried. Remember that prescription drugs are often made from plants so herbal remedies can

still be dangerous. Read the instructions and, kids, tell an adult if you are going to try one of these.

16. Try to relax. I have tried relaxation tapes and exercises where I have to think of each muscle separately and tense it as much as possible, then relax it. You are meant to start at the top of your body and do this for your eyes and everything, and then work downwards. I got bored and my mind started wandering so I found this very difficult. It may work for you, so give it a go. Apparently it takes a lot of practice, so persevere.

17. Massage is also meant to relax people. You never know, you may be lucky enough to find some fit girl (or boy if you are a girl) that is willing to rub massage oil into your body. I know – in your dreams!!

18. Did you know that lettuce is meant to be a natural sedative? I must admit I have never chomped my way through one at bedtime!

19. I know I sound like an adult here, but fresh air and exercise are meant to help people sleep. You have to admit that we do all tend to be computer nerds!

20. I do Taekwondo so this helps me and as I get higher up the ranks it may teach me to relax more too. I can't stress enough how good martial arts are for kids like us.

Sleeping solutions – tips for parents

It's hard for me to give tips here because it depends on the age and ability of your child as to exactly what may work for them. I can give a few tips, though, because I remember when I was younger and I see my Mum with my brothers and they are younger and less able than me. I hope some of these tips may help.

1. Dietary changes help masses and masses of people to sleep better and they are certainly worth investigating. The gluten- and casein-free diet has helped thousands of people to get rid of their sleeping problems. Please look into it though. It is one of the biggest factors in my opinion.

2. I know I have mentioned this for older people, but blackout curtains are even more important for young children. Joe just couldn't sleep ever without them. These are very important.

3. Any annoying sounds in yours or your child's room can prevent sleep. AS people tend to be far more sensitive to noise and smells.

4. A lot of people have difficulty with their body temperature and maybe this is causing a problem getting to or staying asleep. Just because your AS or autistic child doesn't tell you that they are too hot or cold, it doesn't meant they are not.

5. Another thing AS and autistic people all need to help them sleep is to be wrapped up in something heavy. Mum always jokes that she can't find any of us in or beds. We all bury ourselves in our quilts and wrap ʲ around us. She says we look like slugs!

6. Tell your child what to do when they go to the ʰ seems so simple but the actual routine of drawiʲ curtains or blind, turning the light off, getting lying down and pulling the quilt over you is ʲ something instinctive to AS people.

7. As I have said to the older people, a step-b probably in pictures for younger kids, is v

they know their routine and can see it clearly, then they are more likely to settle.

8. Routine, too, is something that is so important for people on the autistic spectrum. Just one toy out of place or cleaning the child's teeth before washing their face can be enough to unsettle them. When I was younger I had a really regimented routine of switching the lights on and off and kissing certain toys (embarrassing to think of now!) and all sorts of other strange things that I won't go into again here.

9. Encourage your child to talk for a while about anything that is on their mind. Maybe even let them draw pictures of the bad times at school or wherever. You write them down and then let them throw them away and be very clear in telling them that the nasty events of the day have now gone.

10. An obvious thing to look at is the amount a child sleeps in the day and what time they go to bed. Try to keep them up later and prevent them from falling asleep in the day, so all their sleep is together. I must say that this didn't work with Joe and Ben. The later they stay up, the more hyper they get.

11. As I have said to the AS people earlier, fresh air and exercise are meant to help someone sleep, so take your child out and exhaust them. It may help.

12. Massage with relaxing oils is really meant to help kids with settling problems. Ben and Joe wouldn't keep still long enough and I don't really fancy the idea, but again, it's worth a try for some, especially for little children.

13. If you have got a child with the sensory problems that Ben has got, then check their pyjamas or quilt cover for labels. Ben can spot a label a mile off and really hates them anywhere near him.

14. However hot it is, don't expect your AS or autistic kid to sleep on top of the quilt because I am pretty sure that there are very few who can sleep without the pressure.

15. A video or television or music playing quietly may help some kids. It wouldn't work for Joe or me but I know it does for some kids. They get distracted and then just doze off.

16. If your child is waking up after getting to sleep then I know people say to leave them to scream for a bit. I know this isn't easy but for a little while I think that you should. I used to try screaming so that I could get out and I remember that.

17. If a child is really screaming and screaming, then I can't see why you shouldn't take them to bed with you. I know they may get used to it, but days and days without sleep for everyone when there is a way of getting sleep seems silly to me. Ben sleeps with Mum all the time now but that's because he is so dangerous and she needs to watch him.

I know all of this may be teaching my granny to suck eggs (go to the back…I bet this one has you baffled!), but there just may be something in here that helps someone. I don't need anywhere near as much sleep as other people and I still have difficulties, but they are better than they were and I do sleep sometimes now. When I am awake I don't wander around the house as much as I used to and I now know that morning will come.

All I can say to you AS kids is keep trying and go down my checklist periodically. What didn't work last week may do this week, or even a year later. Things do change.

Parents, I know it must be hard – I have seen Ben be such a pain (and I guess I am one myself!), but believe me when I say that we just can't help it. In a frightening world, I can't blame Ben and other small kids for not wanting to be dragged away into the unknown. As yet he doesn't know that place is called sleep and will allow him back here later. I, of course, am a cool teenager and have no such fears…well maybe only little ones!

8

Language and Learning

Teenage talk

'She went out with him last night and...'

'No way!'

'I am not kidding, she told me he goes...and she...'

That's a 'conversation' I was listening to recently. My sister was talking to her friend and I watched avidly. I say watched because, as you can see, there were very few words and the whole conversation consisted of them rolling their eyes, flicking their hair, pulling strange faces and laughing.

AS teenagers, would you agree with me that this is one of the most infuriating things about AS when it comes to working out girls? Girls, I am sure you must have the same problem with boys, but I do think that girls seem to be more elaborate in their body language and facial expressions.

At the moment I am trying very hard to be a cool teenager with my spiky hair and my trendy clothes. In my heart of hearts I am by no means a conformist, but at this stage in my life all I want to do is uh hum...pull a few girls – actually just one would be nice! For all AS kids, this difficulty with language, body language and facial expressions is a big one. These are the things that we have massive difficulties with. For the adolescent and teenage person with AS, deciphering other kids' meanings is harder than deciphering ancient hieroglyphics.

Sarah

Teenagers have lots of strange words and they change a lot too. I use some of them myself because I get used to hearing these at school and some are quite good words. I am talking about words like 'minging', 'pants', 'top' and those kind of words. Ben often says 'yats minging' ('yat' means 'that' in Ben's language) and I have to agree that that one does have a good sound to it.

As I have said before, my sisters often say, 'You are such a freak'. Now even though that may sound terribly insulting to most people, that is just their way of talking. It seems to me that non-AS people have their particular way of talking and AS and autistic people have theirs. As usual, because we are in the minority, we are the ones who are misunderstood and ridiculed!

I try to be very polite – I always have been. Mum has taught us all to say please and thank you and to try to be kind to others since we were very little. I don't want to sound boastful, but most people say that I am very polite. This often gets me ridiculed. Isn't that odd? Apparently being very polite means I am a freak. It seems that at my age it is cool to swear for no apparent reason and punctuate most of your sentences with inappropriate obscenities.

I am not saying that I am a saint and that I don't swear. As much as I don't like it, I have to admit that I do when I am angry or hurt myself. I think that most people do, or at least replace the swear word with something similar. If someone says 'shine on' or 'sugar' when they hurt themselves, it is obvious which word they are thinking. To say I am going to the !$*%#@* shops or something similar seems ridiculous and shows a bad command of English and I for one never want to talk like that. I would get in masses of trouble at home anyway. In fact I wouldn't be able to speak at all because my mouth would be so full of soap that I would be blowing bubbles for weeks!

Sarah

I like the English language and like learning new words and speaking correctly. One thing about the way I speak is very strange. Even though I can read perfectly well and understand the meanings of masses of words, it seems that I pronounce a lot of them wrong. Do any of you do that? I am always being laughed at for it. When I was writing this, I was wondering why and all I can think is that people with AS don't spend as much time listening to other people carefully and get more of their vocabulary from books, which of course don't tell you how to pronounce things. I could be wrong of course but…uh hum…I seldom am!

There are some really interesting words and it is fascinating how just to change one word in a sentence can change the whole meaning of that sentence. Even to change an emphasis does that apparently. Here is an example:

- *I* can't do that… implies that I can't, but maybe someone else can.

- I *can't* do that… implies it is not possible.

- I can't do *that*… implies that I can't do that, but may be able to do something else.

Do any of you AS people have difficulty understanding this? I certainly do!

I am told that I put an emphasis on the wrong words sometimes and change the meaning when I don't actually want to. This often means I am misunderstood or misunderstand others. This causes loads of arguments because I am always being told off for saying something wrong when most of the time I don't even know I have. I think picking up on these finer aspects of language may be a problem to a lot of AS people. They are the subtleties that we seem to miss. Wouldn't you AS readers agree?

Have you ever been told to do something like 'Go away for a second while I talk to Uncle Bob or Aunt Doris (I don't mean your Mum has said those names specifically, they are just an example) and you have come back in a second later, much to the exasperation of your Mum? I think a lot of times, other people try not to hurt an AS person's feelings so they are not explicit enough about their own 'rules'. Mum is very blunt with me and I think that shocks other people. She will say, 'Luke shut up for five minutes' (but then she moans when I time five minutes and start again!), or scream, 'Stop poking me.' This doesn't offend me one bit as we all have our own ways and we should try to accept each other.

Does this kind of scenario sound familiar to any of you? Me sitting daydreaming of…well I won't give away all my secrets, but let's just say I am thinking of something far more interesting than maths! All of a sudden, a shadow looms over me. I glance up and see the formidable form of the teacher. He towers over me, arms folded, the pungent mixture of sweat and after-shave filling my nostrils. I await the moment when he pounces. 'Jackson,' he suddenly booms, 'Would you care to tell us exactly where you are?'

'Class E2, Sir,' I respond as quickly and politely as possible.

'Are you trying to be smart?' he snarls, his face reddening with anger.

'Yes, Sir,' I reply, 'of course I am trying to be smart.' I think to myself, 'Surely that is why we are at school?' I breathe an inward sigh of relief, presuming he will now leave me alone, but when I look up, I see I am wrong.

His eyes are bulging, he is breathing fast and hard and his face is the colour of a beetroot. 'Jackson, I will not, I repeat not, tolerate such insolence. You can pull your socks up or get to the headmaster's office.'

Now when I was younger I would have bent down and done just that, pulled my socks up. I know Joe would do just that now. However, I smile to myself inwardly. 'Ha,' I think, 'I know this one – it means get on with your work, not pull your socks up.' Grinning with delight at the fact that I have finally understood, I pick up my pen and start to write. Well you would have thought that that was the end but it seems not!

'This is no laughing matter and how dare you ignore me when I am speaking to you?' Eh? Speaking? I wasn't aware he was? His rage seems to have been replaced by simmering anger that he has managed to suppress only to allow it to erupt at a later date. His face is like thunder. 'See me after class for an hour's detention,' he hisses in my ear in a menacing manner.

For some people on the autistic spectrum, an understandable reaction to the above scenario would be to lose your temper and generally have a screaming abdab at the unfairness of the whole, frustrating situation. I think a lot of younger kids do that and maybe older ones too. As we get older, however, we have to learn to control our tempers and not react like that. Count to ten in your head, think a pleasant thought, work out how many hours til you get home and promise yourself a treat for when you get there. The thought of spending a couple of hours on my computer or on the PlayStation gets me through many a grotty day.

I know that teachers should learn to control their tempers too and often they do not. I know that they should try to understand us more and often they do not. One thing certain in this life is that it is not always fair – it seems as if there is one rule for them and one for us. My advice is to stick to the rules as best as you can.

On the subject of rules, I am sure that all of you AS teenagers have been given some rules on how to behave appropriately. Have you heard of these?

- Don't 'invade people's space' – that means get too close to them.

- Don't stare at someone for whatever reason (however fit they are!).

- Don't make comments about people's bodies, good or bad.

- Don't tell dirty, sexist or racist jokes or make sexual innuendos.

- Don't hug or touch people unless they are part of your family or they have agreed to be your boyfriend or girlfriend and you have both agreed to do it.

If you haven't heard any of those rules, then now you have! Here comes the but...you just watch and listen to a group of teenage boys or girls. First, they will either huddle up together really close or tower over someone in a threatening way. Next they make all sorts of rude comments about the size of people's uh hum...what can I say?! They tell dirty jokes and make sexual innuendos at every opportunity and they will often touch someone or put their arm around them, when they are not a member of their family, their boyfriend or girlfriend.

If these are the rules, then it seems that when boys are girls are in their teenage packs, performing their adolescent rituals, then these rules go out of the window. What a strange world we live in! All in all I would say to stick to the rules and ignore the fact that others seem to be breaking them.

Literalism and logic

Ever since I was little I have used long words and been quite articulate. Mum said that I used to say that playgroup was 'actually rather boring'! I was only around two years old at the time so I suppose that did sound odd.

Ben is different to me in that respect as he has only just started talking and is still not that easy to understand. I think that may be one of the differences between autism and Asperger Syndrome. I have noticed that since he started to talk a bit better, he is very good at mimicking tones of voice, like Joe is, whereas everyone says my voice drones on and is flat. I can't comment on my own voice because I am used to it. People do say that this is one of the things that has changed about me since the diet though (sorry to harp on about this).

Ben is very, very literal in his understanding. Just a few minutes ago I said 'My head is pounding' and Ben happened to be focused on me. He giggled and said 'No not' and started pulling my head around. We have to be very careful not to say 'He cried his eyes out' or expressions like that, as he gets very upset and starts gouging his eyes. Whilst it is good that we have these odd times where he is listening to what we say, he has great difficulty understanding and we have to be very careful what we say around him because he gets very confused. Maybe those of you with AS kids need to be the same.

If we say a word that Ben doesn't understand whilst we have something in our hand, he presumes we are naming the object and will then call that object that word forever more. People think that is funny but it is very confusing for him. Mum was doing some work with him and was saying 'hexagon' and pointing to the shape. However, she was also holding a cup of tea, so now whenever he sees that particular cup he says hexagon! This was over a year ago and he still does it. Once, ages ago, the educational psychologist was testing his ability to mimic and put a plastic, circular pressure pad (off one of those massage things) on her head and then sneezed dramatically so that it fell off – the pressure pad, not her head of course! Ben *did* mimic that and has done so every time he sees anything round and the same colour ever since.

A lot of people seem to think that AS people do and say the most nonsensical things. I must say that people who don't have AS do many things that don't make sense to me!

AS adolescents, I am afraid that I am going to lapse into one of my 'I remember when I was little' moments. I am sure that there are plenty of parents reading this who want to learn about their child before they reach adolescence and all of its joys so please bear with me!

One reason we don't seem to make sense to others is because AS people think very, very logically. As I have said, people with AS take language very literally so what may seem logical to them may not be to someone else. I have had many instances of this in my life. In fact there was one instance where I seemed to be lost, but actually I didn't get lost at all.

Yet Another 'Getting Lost' Story

I was only around five or six and Mum had come to pick me up from school. Eventually a worried headmistress came out and said she needed a word with Mum. Mum was told not to worry (I am sure that wasn't very comforting), but that the school were having difficulty finding me. Apparently my teacher was in a right old state and everyone had been searching for a long time. Knowing a bit about how I thought, Mum asked what was the last thing the teacher had said to me. The teacher replied that she had told me to put my file back under her desk. Understanding my ways, Mum quickly looked under the desk and there I was.

Now here is my version of the event. Mrs Reidy said, 'Luke could you nip under my desk [the desk was pretty big and I was pretty small] and put your file back?' I obeyed and crawled under the desk and replaced the file into the big box. I like being underneath things. It gives me a feeling of warmness as if I am safe. The confusing world seems remote and surreal when I have something overhead or am enclosed in something. Despite the enjoyable feeling of being enclosed beneath the desk, I was actually only being obedient. The teacher didn't say, 'Luke nip under the desk, put your file back and come out.' She said, 'Nip under the desk.' Nobody actually told me I was supposed to come out again!

Mum is very particular about people saying what they mean and being clear. She is so good with words and gets really annoyed if we say she means something other than what she really does. She will say, 'I am quite capable of speaking clearly enough. I have just said exactly what I mean.' Don't beat around the bush. Ever heard that one?

A big part of autistic spectrum disorders is a problem with communication. That is why language causes AS people so many problems. Non-AS people say things they don't mean, miss out things that they do mean, do all sorts of strange things with their faces which apparently change the meaning of their words – and they say AS people are odd!

To say 'If you do so-and-so (not literally of course) then it makes me feel sad and I do not like feeling sad so please do not do it again' is fine and simple to understand (and of course any varia-tion on that), but adults and people in general usually go on about 'How do you think this makes me feel?' and 'Do you not care about us?' and 'You are so selfish' and I still end up wondering exactly what the point is that they are trying to make!

I am always being shouted at for not thinking of what others may be feeling, but I am sorry to say that I often do not. I have great difficulty thinking what others may be feeling and, even when they tell me, they are never clear enough. I think people should be very clear to AS people.

People with AS often seem to talk slowly or in a monotonous voice. I personally can't hear this but I know that my sisters notice it and say that it seems to be true of many – of course not all, because we are not clones after all! I tend to speak very slowly (which bugs people no end) but that's just the way I am. I think people get bored with listening to me but I don't usually notice unless they tell me, so it is not a problem – not for me anyway! Some AS people just take a while for their brain to process thoughts and anyone around them should be patient and realize that this doesn't mean that they are slow in their minds, just that things take a while.

Precise parents make cheerful children

Now, before any of you clear, precise-speaking parents with unhappy children get straight on to my publisher and give her a piece of your mind, I do know that life is not quite as simple as that! As much as I have no trouble writing, the subheadings in this book seemed to have been on the tip of my tongue (or fingers) and are sticking there like stubborn ulcers! More often than not, I have opted for the alliteration avenue (there – I am doing it again!) for want of any better option.

If any of you have AS children of any age and you can't quite fathom them out, then think carefully about how you speak. Do you really explain yourself clearly enough? If you give an instruction, you should never presume that the child automatically knows what you mean. Things that seem obvious to you do not to us and our logic may be different to others'. AS people really do like you to call a spade a spade (that one is really silly, as if we would call it anything else!).

As I have illustrated, most AS kids are very literal, but as we get older we learn to understand these obscure ways of speaking. We also learn which phrases mean what and even use them appropriately ourselves. The difference between us and non-AS kids is that these are things that we have to make an effort to learn, whereas it seems that such things come naturally to other kids. A bit unfair having even more to learn in life than others, but hey, that's life and we should just get on with it – no point crying over spilled milk. See I told you we could learn to use them appropriately!

If you have an AS kid or know an AS person, then don't presume that they can automatically read the insinuations in your language. If you want them to and think it is important, then teach them. The same goes with things that seem trivial like tidying up. These aren't trivial to Mum. She gets really bugged about us lot making such a mess. She wanders around muttering to herself about how we think there is no point having a dog and barking ourselves. We don't have a dog! I had to go and look that one up because when she says that it is *not* a good time to ask for meanings – though one thing I will say about Mum is her bark is worse than her bite!

Parents, don't scream at your kids to tidy their bedrooms if you haven't explained exactly what tidy up means. I know that a lick and a promise isn't good enough (Ben brings a whole new meaning to that one!). If the instructions are clear – first pick up the dirty clothes, then put them in the linen bin, and all that kind of stuff – then at least the child has something specific to do (and then they can still ignore you!).

I often wander around my room wondering where to start. Checklists and charts are good for that kind of stuff. The same goes for washing and personal hygiene. Explain to them exactly how to wash their hair and their body and exactly how many times they have to change their underwear. Now this certainly

Sarah

doesn't mean that they will then be clean and tidy. Ha! Chance would be a fine thing, Mum will now be saying! Without these explanations, though, there will be no chance at all. I have to admit that, even with specific instructions, washing and stuff like that are not a top priority in my life. I always feel as if I am doing it for the benefit of others because personally I don't care whether I am clean or dirty and don't care what other people think about me either. This is something that I am trying to change, purely and simply because I have read my own dating chapter!! Here are a few more tips on how to teach your child the ways of the world.

1. Give clear and specific instructions about what you want your child to do.

2. Avoid using similes and particularly metaphors unless you can explain them accurately.

3. Don't ever presume that your child can pick up the rights and wrongs of certain behaviours along the course of his or her life.

4. All things need to be spelled out clearly to any child, but a child on the autistic spectrum needs things spelled out to them more than most. In a way they are like foreigners.

5. Teach them about the value of money and the rights and wrongs of taking other people's things. Explain clearly that this is a rule.

6. You need to tell AS kids that others will be sad and angry if their property is taken and use illustrations from the past so that the child can identify with how the other person may feel.

7. Explain things in a way that is very clear and use comparisons that your own child is likely to understand. Analogies from their specialist subject will capture their attention.

8. Keep checking things over with your AS kid to make sure they have understood.

I am sure there are far more tips on the problems with language in other books but I am writing from my perspective, looking into the past and the problems I have now…and after all…I am only thirteen!

9

The Problem with School...

For any kid, whether they enjoy it or not, school is a whole mine-field of challenges and new experiences. I remember Mum saying that when we all started school we would be exhausted by the time we came home and be so bad-tempered. For kids on the autistic spectrum it seems as if we spend all of our time stepping on these mines (don't worry, any kids reading this, there are no mines really – I am just using metaphors) and the whole school experience becomes a very difficult one.

How many of you AS adults reading this remember having a good time at school? If I were a gambling person, then I would bet that most if not all of you said 'No way' to that one! Many older AS people that I have talked to tell me that school memories range from being best forgotten to impossible to forget because they were so traumatic. This is all wrong and any of us who are still in any school system should set about educating teachers, other kids, parents and anyone else who can help to change such things.

When I was in the junior school I had all sorts of problems with bullying, sound sensitivity (why on earth they have to deafen everyone with a bell, numerous times a day, I will never know!), understanding exactly what I was meant to be doing, forgetting stuff and being too slow at most things. AS kids, I am presuming that you all have similar kind of problems?

At school everything changes so often. I am not totally locked into routines and Mum tries hard to change things regularly so that Ben doesn't become that way either, but still, going into a classroom to find that we then have to join another class because the teacher is off, or move desks for no apparent reason, all adds to the hassle of school.

Everything is so busy at school and everyone else, all the kids and all the teachers, seems to have a purpose and I never have quite fathomed out what that purpose is. I know we are there to learn, but there seems to be so much more going on than that. It is like beginning a game without knowing any of the rules or passwords.

For any classroom assistants or professionals or teachers reading this, then please, please try to realize that instinctively knowing where to go and who to talk to and what to do next just isn't possible for a kid on the autistic spectrum. If a teacher says 'now get out your books and turn to page 10' and doesn't say 'and now start answering those questions', then the AS kid is not likely to know; so to tell them off for doing no work that lesson is unfair.

I have lost count of the number of times I have been told to copy a title off the blackboard and then sat patiently waiting for what to do next, whilst everyone else scribbled frantically. Only later, as a teacher wanders around the classroom like a hungry animal, carefully selecting the tastiest morsel, do I usually become the unfortunate prey as I get pounced upon with a barrage of 'Jackson, why are you sat doing nothing?' and 'Get on with your work, boy'. Teachers and support assistants *please* tell the AS kids exactly what they are expected to get on with.

I used to have a teacher who helped me at school, but at the time I didn't have a clue what she helped me with. Teaching assistants, whatever level of understanding the child you are working

Rachel

with has got, then I reckon you should still try to involve the child so that they know what is going on.

I also used to have an occupational therapist come into school and do stuff like making me stand on one leg and lie on the floor and scrunch my toes together and then relax them and throw beanbags at boards. One minute I was sat in a classroom and the next I was carted off to the hall with a few other kids to do this kind of stuff. No one ever told me why! I was quite glad to do this kind of stuff rather than do lessons – what kid wouldn't be? It was quite unsettling, though, to get used to what I was doing and then suddenly have to change.

I know I am repeating myself (something I tend to do a lot, as my sisters will tell you!), but I will say again that the key to helping a child on the autistic spectrum is to always make sure you tell them very clearly what is going on. I really cannot stress this enough. The same applies all through an AS person's life. If you explain to them clearly in terms that you may even consider below their intelligence, it really does help. I can breathe such a sigh of relief when I know exactly what is going on and why. AS people, make sure you tell your teachers and assistants this.

Reading, writing and 'rithmetic

Reading

Some people on the autistic spectrum learn to read extremely early without ever being taught. This is called hyperlexia and I know nothing at all about it so all I can do is include a link at the back. When Mum or Granny talks about my Uncle Colin, it sounds as if he may have had this. He read newspapers and stuff like that fluently, way before he went to school. If he were assessed now he would probably be classed as dyspraxic like me too. He still has trouble riding a bike and tying shoelaces and Mum says he was always so clumsy. He is a director of a communications company now and is super clever and everyone likes him so if I have inherited my genes (not the denim ones) from him, then I will be well pleased.

My elder brother Matthew is dyslexic. It seems as if that is often found in the family of people with autism. He jumbles words around and has real trouble spelling anything. Mum paid loads of money to a private tutor in the hope that someday he would just click. It took three years for her to click and realize that he wasn't going to! There are word processors with spellchecks and dyslexic dictionaries and all sorts to help people with this problem. There are also glasses called Irlen lenses which I know help many people. I have included links about all this at the back. I won't say much more as I don't have this problem so I only know what I have read or seen in Matthew. By the way, Matthew got 7 GCSEs and has nearly finished a course that is the equivalent to A levels, so that shows it can be done. It was not without a struggle but he got there.

Reading was not something that I did at an early age but I did have some problems with reading when I was younger. The school gave me all sorts of extra help with reading and I couldn't even remember one letter from the other. However much anyone taught me, it just would not sink in. I had had an assessment by an educational psychologist when I was seven years and eight months old and my reading age was not assessable because I just couldn't read anything. The next day Mum got a phone call from the school asking her to come in and see them.

She told me that she was very worried as that usually meant that I was having a massive tantrum, but when she got there the teachers had something that they just couldn't wait to tell. I had picked up a copy of *A Midsummer Night's Dream*, which the teacher was using to show how plays were written. It seems that I opened the book and began to read it fluently. How weird is that?! I wonder if that has a name too – 'can't-read-then-suddenly-starts-to-lexia' maybe? Hypo is the opposite of hyper so it may be something to do with that.

The educational psychologist came and assessed me again on that day too because she was so interested. My reading age then came out at fourteen years and ten months. I am just thirteen now and my reading age was assessed at seventeen years and nine months. I haven't a clue how they decide on that kind of stuff but I suppose any psychologists reading this will know. I hope there are some!

I hope this encourages parents never to give up on a child who seems unable to learn to read. I told Mum and school that someone had 'switched a light on in my head'. Maybe this happens in other areas and at different ages with people, so never give up trying. Now I read lots of books and have read forty-five just this term. I

won an award for that at school. How easy was that one! I read
Harry Potter and the Goblet of Fire in one night. I now have the
electric switched off at night time because otherwise I read and
read and read and never go to sleep. Strange how things work out.

Books are my doorways into other worlds. They cheer me
when I am upset; they make me laugh, cry and quake with fright.
A good book should keep someone entranced right till the end. I
am not sure whether mine will do that as they are factual. I will try,
though.

I am afraid I cannot really give any decent advice on how to
teach your AS child to read as I did it in such a strange way. I do
know, though, that people on the autistic spectrum respond much
better to visual stuff and may be more likely to memorize the look
of whole words than learn to 'build' them. Building words with
sounds was a concept I never did grasp. Neither did Joe, but he has
just clicked at exactly the same age as me. Ben is nowhere near
reading, he can't even count or recognize letters yet, but it will be
interesting to see if he is the same age when he clicks also.

Teachers and support workers who are trying to teach a child
on the autistic spectrum to read, if all else fails then leave them in a
room with one book that may be of interest to the child. It may be
that they too just have something 'switched on' in their heads.
Most AS people enjoy things much more when they are doing it
themselves.

We tried everything to teach Ben how to use a computer mouse
and to show him that moving the mouse was linked to what was
going on on the screen. No way could he understand that, but at
three o'clock in the morning, when Mum was tired out, she lay on
the couch and left him sat up to the computer and he just worked it
out for himself. He now has the most amazing mouse control and
can find his favourite web page, send emails (even though they

only say 44444 – his favourite number) and do way more things than a lot of people can do.

One thing I could not do is tell a story just by looking at a picture. I think this is a really stupid concept. I remember one assessment where the educational psychologist drew a man and asked me to say what he was doing. 'Duh – it is just pen and paper', I told her scornfully! To me, asking me to do this is like asking a person to paint a picture but yet giving them no brushes or paint.

I must say that not all AS or autistic kids are the same, though. I can think of at least one kid with a diagnosis of AS who has the most ridiculously wild imagination ever. He is called Sam and is so much like Joe and they run around like mad things together at Blackpool Bears (that's our disabled sport session at Blackpool Sports Centre). One minute they are crawling around snapping at people's ankles and are crocodiles and the next they are leaping off chairs and are monkeys. Notice that I haven't said 'pretending to be a monkey or a crocodile' – when they are doing this they seem to really think that they are these animals. Since we have met Sam, he has been so many characters that I am not sure if we have ever met the real him at all!

The author Marilyn Le Breton's son Jack is diagnosed as autistic but he too has this crazy, wild imagination and most nights Marilyn herself has to be some superhero to fit in with Jack's roles (not that you are not a superhero anyway, Marilyn!). I think teachers and doctors have a problem with this when they work with an autistic or AS child as we are supposed to have no imagination. Mine really does seem to be very limited and I am a very factual person, but generally I think that AS kids do have imaginations. AS people would you agree?

It seems as if it is all to do with the intensity of their role-playing again. AS or autistic kids seem to take things to extremes. I have seen Joe and Sam act out the most amazing scenarios and insist that everyone else joins in. I know that Jack Le Breton does this too. I think this overactive imagination is a form of escapism. Ben has started to 'be' a dog lately. He barks and crawls and carries things around in his mouth. This seems to be when he is stressed.

All this just goes to show just how much these diagnoses cross over and link with each other. There is a book called *Reweaving the Autistic Tapestry* by Lisa Blakemore-Brown which goes on about how all these diagnoses are interlinked. People with AS can have AD/HD, people with AD/HD can have a lot of similarities with AS but be very hyper and have attention problems – and so it goes on. I have said loads of times that no two people are exactly the same, AS or not.

Here are some tips for any AS kids that hate being taught to read and are not interested in books. I realize that this is a massive contradiction in terms because if you are reading this, then you can already read so this is unnecessary!

Teenagers, I reckon you are bored stiff by now but try to put up with this and remember how it was for you when you were younger and were feeling lost in the world (even more than you do now!).

Parents of AS or autistic kids – could you read this bit out to your child please? It may help them.

1. Kids – you really are missing out and will so love the world of books when you get started.

2. Listen carefully when you are being taught and don't disappear into your own head or start twiddling with things when you don't understand.

3. Tell your teacher or parent, over and over again, when you don't understand.

4. Look at the shape of the words and letters and try to memorize them and what they mean.

5. Look at books with lots of pictures in and pick ones that look fun. You must realize that the words are to do with the pictures that you see.

6. Instead of sitting at your computer or messing with your Pokémon cards, ask your parents or Mum to get a simple book that is about these things and just look at it and realize that books and words will help you learn more about your favourite topic.

7. Get rid of all the adults around you and just have a good look at these things and try to dredge back from your memory the lessons you have had on letter sounds and the way words are formulated.

8. Relax and enjoy looking at books and pictures and having stories read to you. You will do it for yourself one day.

Good luck. Soon you too may be getting in trouble for reading too much. Adults are never satisfied!

Writing

Writing is something that I find very difficult. Holding a pen makes my hand ache and what I actually think never quite appears the same on paper. This used to get me very mad and I would go through masses and masses of paper writing just one little bit and then screwing it up and chucking it away. The same can be said for drawing. I suppose I like things to be perfect and my writing certainly isn't.

I know you may consider it to be a waste of paper if your child or the person you are working with is doing this, but I am afraid that the only solution may be to get some cheap paper. It is impossible to carry on working on one piece of paper whilst there is something wrong staring you in the face on another bit of the paper. Maybe you could encourage the person to turn the paper over and use the back, but that is not possible in exercise books of course.

Rachel

At school I use a word processor now and that is so much easier. I know that everyone has to be able to write a bit but so many doctors and professional people write terribly, so it cannot be that important to write neatly. My Mum writes like a little child and she absolutely hates doing it and she has a degree and all sorts of other qualifications.

Parents, if your child is very slow and struggling to get their work done, then buying them a word processor to use may be the answer. Ideally, the school should provide it and any teachers reading this please realize this is important and not just laziness.

Most AS kids relate better to computers than people so working on a laptop or word processor will enable them to work better and faster. If you are not sure about this, then give them a chance to show you. You will be very surprised.

Any AS kids reading this, don't use this as any excuse never to write again because you do need to be able to write in life, but it will make your life easier. If you are worried about being teased and being different, then I find that strange because I am sure you are pretty different anyway. Remember different is cool!

'Rithmetic

I don't really mean arithmetic here, but maths in general. I can't say a lot about this at all. It is something that I had loads of difficulty with when I was younger and now I just plod away at it. I am no genius in this area but a lot of AS kids are. It seems to be one thing that you either excel at or you don't. (I suppose that is a silly statement, though, because that applies to most things in life.)

A lot of kids with AS love Latin, German and definitely information technology (IT). There may be some subjects which are better suited to an AS person's brain but, generally speaking, we are not clones and have our own strengths and weaknesses. Despite the film *Rain Man*, we don't all have these amazing mathematical skills – I wish!

Not to mention homework

I would really rather not mention it actually – in fact I would like not to think about it and I would most definitely rather not do it! Don't you agree, AS kids? However, as most of you reading this book are either in the same boat as myself (I know – there is no boat!), have kids that are in the same position as myself or are working with a kid like myself, then I will mention homework

Homework Prohibited

Rachel

after all. If you are a teacher reading this, then you may not like what I have to say!

First of all – what do we go to school to do? Duh…schoolwork, of course! I know a lot of people will go on about teamwork and social skills and organization skills and I think I have said my views on that already, but generally the main part of school is to do lessons. We are there to do schoolwork.

Now, I may be a little stupid here or schools in my area may be massively different to other areas (I actually know that they are not because I have talked to other people on the internet), but at the end of lessons the teachers tell us to get our homework diaries out and write down that we must finish the work we have started in class. If they don't tell us to do that, then we have to do Exercise 7G questions 1–19, for example. Yes, you guessed it…all this stuff is out of our 'school' textbooks. We are told to look on the internet for stuff when we could easily do that at school. All in all, 'homework' is identical to 'schoolwork' – the only difference being that it is done at home!

Why is this? I tend to think it's because the world is full of nonsensical, illogical rubbish. Surely, if we have a certain amount of work to cover, then school is the place to do it? Are we being taught self-discipline or being tested to see if we can work alone? If so, then that is completely false because, for all the school knows, we could be getting other people to do it for us anyway. Teachers even tell us to ask our parents for help if we are stuck. What good will that do us?

Teachers tell us that all they want to do is get school kids ready for the big exams because they will count for so much in later life. If you have a good education and a good lot of GCSEs and A levels, you will almost undoubtedly be able to get the job you want. Does any of this sound familiar? Has this convinced you of the need for homework? Nope, I thought not – me neither! Where is the logic in letting us flounder about doing work on our own when the object of the exercise is for us to learn the stuff properly? If we are to do an hour and a half in the evening, then why not make the school day that much longer? Why not make the dinner break shorter, rather than leaving us to hang around for well over an hour wondering what to do with ourselves?

I wonder whether this is to do with the length of time teachers want to work and even maybe the length of time the government wants to pay them. The more work they do, the more they have to get paid so it is cheaper to get us to work at home. Some kind of child labour maybe? I thought all that stopped years ago!

I think that our time at home should be just that – time at home. We have to go to school. The law says we have to go to school or at least be educated otherwise. I have written about that further on and it is an important bit for you all to read. At the moment, though, I will presume most of you or your kids go to school.

School is hard for anyone. There is a lot to remember, a lot to organize and a lot to learn. That applies to kids without any difficulties. For kids with AS or any kind of difficulty, it is even harder because we have to work at stuff that comes naturally to others. I don't think that anyone would expect someone with one leg to be able to keep up with everything that two-legged people were doing, but yet people with AS are expected to keep up with everything at school and very few allowances are made. I know I sound like a sulky kid, but it's all very unfair...stamps foot and sticks bottom lip out here!

There are many days when I have great difficulty remembering what I am meant to be doing from one minute to the next. I get distracted very easily and things that are important to others often don't seem so to me and vice versa. For kids with attention problems it must be really, really difficult. Joe often can't remember what anyone has said to him a second afterwards, so how on earth is he meant to remember what homework to do, or even that he has got any? He cannot remember to write it in his diary unless he is reminded and then forgets to bring his bag or his diary home anyway.

Once at home, Joe sits down at a table with the stuff he is meant to do in front of him. He then keeps getting up and flicking his pencil around and can't sit still. Mum ends up getting in a bad mood and shouts, 'Will someone see if they can help Joe to do his homework?' So another of us takes over and so it goes on. All in all it takes literally hours. Poor Joe really tries hard too. I feel very sorry for him with stuff like this. He is trying really hard at the moment.

When Joe comes in from school he likes to run up and down the hall and shriek like a monkey and do 'midgy men'. This is where he does manic bunnyhops and covers his knees in bruises. He has way too much energy when he comes in and Mum just lets him go mad for quite a while before she shouts, 'That's enough' and we all breathe a sigh of relief. I am the opposite. I like to sit and read or, best of all, play on the PlayStation or go on my laptop.

For some reason, Mum has a real problem with that and we always have the 'Have you got any homework?' and 'Hang on, I will check' routine! I then get out my homework diary, look all meaningful and say 'No, I did it in the library' or 'Yes, but it doesn't have to be in for another week'. I am now going to let myself in for a load of trouble but when I get out that little diary I very often haven't written in it anyway!

I cannot keep up with the speed at which the teachers tell us what to write. I am too busy trying to pack away and worrying about where I am going next to do that kind of stuff too. Sometimes I do write stuff down, but I scribble it so quickly that I cannot read it or it just doesn't make sense.

I suppose I should now give advice on how to cope with having homework and how to make it easier to do. I must say that this really does bug me because I feel as if I am accepting and even contributing to something that I think is very wrong. As far as I am concerned, home is home and school is school and never the twain should meet. So, here it comes. Advice on how to cope with homework. First and foremost, go right to your headmaster and give him a piece of your mind…snigger. Don't do this really or you will get into trouble. I feel as if I want to give out tips to help all you AS kids avoid doing homework but we are stuck with it, so here are some tips that will ease it slightly. (and only slightly!).

Doing homework – ways to make the best out of a bad job

1. Try to arrange to do your homework in the library at dinner or stay late after school to do it. This works best for me. It is schoolwork we are doing after all.

2. If you can't do the work at school, then maybe you could swap houses with someone and do your work

there. I find that doing homework anywhere other than home is best.

3.   If you have to do it at home, then take a deep breath and tell your parent that they are not to let you do anything else til your homework is done (and be prepared for battle when you don't want them to enforce this).

4.   Set up your own 'homework' area and make sure no one interferes with it.

5.   Try to incorporate homework into part of your routine rather than sitting and feeling resentful that it has to be done.

6.   Try to think of it as revising rather than an extension of schoolwork. This makes it more acceptable because, horrible as it is, we have to revise for exams. Teachers can only teach us, not learn for us.

Not much fun and games

If I have succeeded in getting even one games teacher to under-stand anything at all about the nature of AS and the difficulties we experience in games, then writing this whole book will have been worthwhile and I really will be on cloud nine. (Ha – I am getting good!) All AS kids reading this make sure that you or your parent shows at least this bit to the games teacher.

I have said loads of times that we are not all the same, so there may be exceptions to this, but I reckon there aren't many. Most AS kids genuinely have a really hard time with games – we are *not* just being lazy. I have never been any good at football or any team sports. I hate them and will do all I can to avoid playing them. There are quite a few reasons for this. I have pretty poor

Rachel

co-ordination and am not very good at catching, throwing, kicking and controlling a ball. OK, OK, I admit it...I am absolutely terrible at catching, throwing, kicking and controlling a ball – I have enough trouble controlling my arms and legs actually!

I don't hang around in a group and everyone is aware of how bad I am at team sports so no one ever wants me in their team. The familiar hustle and bustle, murmuring and giggling that follow the instruction 'Get into teams' are always accompanied by the predictable 'Aw Sir, do we have to?' or 'No way are we having him' as the games teacher allocates me to a random team, rather like a spare piece of luggage that no one can be bothered to carry. I tell you their feelings are reciprocated – no way do I want to be in their team either!

Another reason why I hate team sports so much is that everyone seems to be running around and screaming and shouting and it is all so disjointed. I cannot work out where the noise is coming from or who it is directed at and it all becomes very confusing and, sorry to sound wimpish, it is very frightening (though of course I am now a cool teenager and so cannot say that!). When I finally work out what I am meant to be doing or where I am meant to be running to, they have started doing something else and everyone is jeering at me for getting it wrong. I have never quite fathomed out what the 'it' is, but whatever it is, it's a pointless one – at least so it seems to me!

Chasing a ball around a pitch seems pretty futile to me. In basketball or a sport like that, someone jumps for a ball and, even if they don't catch it, everyone cheers. All very strange! It's at these times that I really do feel as if I come from another planet and, to be quite honest, I like mine better. Beam me up, Scotty!

People pay players millions of pounds to kick a ball around and people travel from country to country just to watch. It also seems as if the world's biggest bullies use football as an excuse to do their bullying in mass proportions – football hooligans. This is all in the name of watching football. Stupid, stupid stuff.

Now I am in secondary school, this sports issue is even worse. I am in a private school and here it seems we are now expected to love talking about rugby or golf. Well, whoopee doo… I would rather watch paint dry. Quite literally. The thought of doing games really makes me feel ill. I can't even think about sleeping at night when I have games the next day. I can't concentrate on the lessons before as my worst nightmare is slowly approaching. When it is time for the lesson, I genuinely do feel sick and have a headache from all the worrying. Of course I am told that I will be able to run it off or just ignored completely. It is my worst time at school and I have done all I can to avoid it.

Body Space

I am really only writing about this because other people tell me I have a problem with it. If that is so, then that could have a lot to do with why I am so rubbish at games. If I can't judge where my body is, then I am not likely to be able to connect it with a ball so well. As I have said before, I am me so some things are hard to judge. Other AS people, how often have you heard someone hiss in exasperation, 'Will you please move up a bit' or 'Stop following me'? Those of course are the polite versions. 'Get lost, you freak' is just as familiar!

I am told that I sit and stand far too close to people and follow them around unnecessarily. This isn't just people like Mum or Sarah who hate to have their personal space invaded; apparently I go too close to everyone. I can't say a lot about this apart from to be aware that it may be a problem. If people tell you that you do this, then get very clear rules as to how close is acceptable to stand and make very sure that you don't get too close to people at school. If you stand too close to a member of your own sex, then you will be called gay, and if you stand too close to the opposite sex, everyone will say that you fancy them. All this kind of stuff is very hard to work out but maybe if you AS kids read that you are not alone, then you may feel a little better.

A note for games teachers

All I can say here is please don't torture us anymore. If you know someone has AS or dyspraxia, then they genuinely have difficulties (understatement) with your subject. When we leave school we are most definitely not going to be footballers, rugby players or any other team players, so is it not possible to find out what we are good at now and some way to help us in that instead?

If someone frequently loses or forgets their games kit (uh hum...not that I ever do that!) or always develops stomach ache, a headache or hurts themselves, then the chances are they are trying to avoid games. I know I am stating the obvious and you already know that, but I just wanted all games teachers to know why. There is always a slim chance that they are genuinely feeling under the weather (I wonder where that one came from?) but it's unlikely.

Please realize that making someone do a team sport is not suddenly going to make him or her become sociable and co-ordinated. In fact it is a pretty daft idea to think that anything at all is going to make an AS person suddenly have no difficulty with social interaction. That is like saying that if a blind person holds a book in front of their nose long enough they are going to suddenly be able to see! Maybe if you are still in doubt, you could put in a set of ear plugs, wear a pair of goggles and try a team sport whilst only allowing yourself to catch or kick the ball with the hand or foot that you are not used to. This is what it feels like all the time for us. It's very difficult isn't it?!

Maybe a lot of us would be in danger of becoming couch potatoes and doing no exercise and I also know that your job is to make sure people have a try at these sports. No one is asking you, as a games teacher, to tell all the people that are avoiding games to go and sit at a computer and I can see the point about computers making people lazy and unfit. Our society is in danger of having a lot of unfit people about.

AS people are often very good at individual sports such as running (remember Forrest Gump?), rock climbing…in fact anything that doesn't involve lots of interaction with others. If the school has a gym, is it not possible for the AS person to go there and work out whilst the others play football or their team sport? I know this must feel like a very defeatist attitude but, believe me, in this area we are defeated! This is a recognized disability and these problems are part of it. It is a fundamental part of who we are, so please try to understand and help us in any way you can.

I don't know about any of the rest of you with AS, but the thought of games even now makes my shoulders droop and my heart sink so I am going to change the subject or I will be too depressed to write any more. Games teachers, I hope you have got the message. Thanks if you have!

School or otherwise – if it still goes wrong

As I have said, a lot of AS and autistic people really struggle at school. AS kids reading this, I reckon that it is some small comfort to know that you are definitely *not* alone.

Ben is in a special school that seems really good for him at the moment. Apparently he doesn't take his clothes off at all and he walks at least most of the time (he crawls when he is feeling insecure), so he must feel fairly confident there. I often wonder what is next for him though. If he is too clever for special schools then how will he cope with the bell going off, the changes in noises from one echoing room to another, the lights being suddenly turned off to watch a video? These are all things that Ben cannot cope with.

Home education is a possibility. It seems that if your child is in mainstream, then you can write a special letter to the school saying that you want to deregister and that is that (get your Mum's signature at the ready, AS kids!). If they are in a special school, you have to write to the local education authority and ask for consent. This of course is how it is in the UK but I do know that people home educate in many different countries. I have put worldwide links at the back.

There are lots and lots of people who home educate and more and more who are doing it with autistic spectrum children. I thought it was against the law. I also presumed that if you could do this then you would have to get a tutor in to the house and have GCSE papers sent to the home – but apparently not. An education plan can be devised that suits the child instead of trying to fit the child into the national curriculum.

This is all new to me and I think it is brilliant for many kids who just will not fit into a school. For some people, it is like fitting a square peg into a round hole. For me at the moment, the hole (the school) has changed its shape slightly to accommodate me and the square peg (me) has tried to soften its edges, so a better description would be a rounded square trying to fit itself into a circle with sticky-out bits! I am in a fee-paying school so I think this is why it may be a little easier now.

A couple of years ago I would have said that I would never have fitted and I am glad that if things get really bad that there is an option. At the moment, though, I just do my work, go from class to class and look forward to home times and weekends. I think I will be able to do my GCSEs there and get along OK, although I can never say I really enjoy school. Does anyone? At least I've gone from hating school to not liking it. There is quite a big difference you know. If things get bad again and it can't be sorted, then the option is there. I have got through many a bad day with that knowledge. I think I must be like one of those people who can give up smoking if they have a cigarette on them as back-up just in case. They never touch it but it is there. At the moment I think I will stay at school, but who knows.

The options are there and there is a book about *Home Educating Our Autistic Spectrum Children*. I have included it in the Further Reading at the back. Many people just don't realize that this is an option. I hope more do now. This is important!

10

Bullying

My experiences

All my life I have been bullied. Well at least I mean periodically and at school, not at home – not literally every minute of my life. That really would be a sad existence! I have found this a very upsetting chapter to write so I hope it helps some of you. I know writing it has made me resolve never to let them get away with it again. If you are being bullied, then you do the same.

I still remember going to nursery (or pink playgroup as I used to call it). My Grandad used to pick me up. I remember people putting stupid outfits on and hats that were too big and I hated it. I used to scream and push people away from me and the other kids used to laugh. That was my first experience of being bullied. I felt different.

When I started school I struggled to understand what was going on, but one thing I did understand was that most of the kids were pretty mean to me. I never knew why. Everything at school was so loud and so complicated then. At my first school I was bullied by one particular group of boys year after year. Whatever punishment the school doled out (which I have to admit wasn't much), whatever course of action Mum or I took, they always started again. They used to push and shove me and call me names and generally try to make my life miserable. Those four boys in particular seemed to make it their lifelong mission to annoy, upset, hurt and aggravate me.

The teachers did try hard (or at least some of them did) but I think Mum did the most good by having a 'quiet word' with these kids. I think when kids are younger, then adults, though not all, intimidate some of them. Mum says that a parent should never take the bullying problem into their own hands but yet she seemed to take kids to one side and even look as though she was smiling when she was talking to them. Maybe it was more of a grimace. I am not good at facial expressions.

I have just asked her what she said to them and she has told me that she tried to reason with them and say that she would tell me to keep away from them if they kept away from me. If it didn't work, I think she told them that she would make them as miserable as they were making me. She assures me that this was not threatening them (though I know it sounds like it) but that she was just saying things in a way that could be open to any interpretation and was leaving the rest to their conscience and imagination. Sorry if this all sounds a bit vague; I am merely repeating what Mum said.

The bullies would leave me alone for some time after that but, even though things were better, I sure was glad to leave that school. Unfortunately I landed in the fire. The secondary school that I went to had a very good reputation and in particular a good reputation where bullying was concerned. That's why my Mum fought so hard to get us in. For me it didn't work out. The bullies there just couldn't be dealt with and no amount of threatening by my brother, by the teachers, the fear of expulsion, pleasant reasoning, absolutely nothing made any difference and they never left me alone. In the end they were physically pushing me around and punching me and it was about the worst time of my entire life.

One day things just got too much to bear. I had tried to hide in the changing rooms away from my tormentors – I wish I had written my book then as I would have realized that hiding away is the worst thing to do. These two lads (lowlifes!) found me and began toying with me in much the same way as a cat plays with a mouse. Pulling and pushing, teasing and cajoling, they seemed to revel in my discomfort. Thinking of nothing but the need to escape from these brainless baboons, I pushed my way past them and kept on running. Through the schoolyard, out of the school gates, I ran and ran but still they pursued me only to finally catch up with me and shower me with kicks and punches. Luckily for me, a man was going to the nearby swimming baths and stopped and got them off me. The two bullies of course ran off. What else would you expect from cowards? I was taken into the swimming baths and they called Mum who came straight to pick me up. I didn't want to call the police or do anything other than leave that school for good. I never did go back to that school again and stayed at home until we decided that I might as well have a try at the private school that I am at now.

I have been bullied here too but it got sorted out very quickly and the kids involved seemed scared at the thought of their parents being brought in. I think maybe that is the difference between going to a private school, which I do now, and going to a state school. Sad but true.

One thing that I can say is that the fact that I do Taekwondo seems to make an impact on other kids. Stupid, I know, but then in my experience bullies are stupid. AS kids, it is worth having a go at Taekwondo or another martial art. It is good for so many aspects of your life. I have only given a brief outline of my experience to show that I am not merely talking about something I know nothing about. Believe me I certainly do!

What is bullying?

Bullying can be a variety of things. Don't think that you are not being bullied just because you may not be getting punched or kicked or physically hurt. Physical bullying is not always so black and white either. (In fact, it is often black and blue! Sorry, that was just a bad joke.) Any form of unwanted touching is physical bullying. Bullying can be in verbal form as well. All this makes it very hard for AS people to work out. I will try to be as clear as possible about this and maybe I can help.

Rachel

Generally I would say that if other people are doing something or saying something to you that hurts or upsets you, then that is bullying. I think this is an important thing for AS kids or maybe even adults to know. Sometimes bullying carries on because someone may not recognize that it is bullying which they are experiencing. No one will ever come up to you and say, 'Now I am going to bully you'. If someone is telling you to do something that you really do not want them to do, or something that is going to get you in trouble or harm you in some way, then that is bullying too.

Since I have been talking about this to my Mum, I have realized that lots of things which have gone on at school that I have just taken for granted are actually forms of bullying too. One thing to remember is that a lot of these things are done very sneakily in order to get the person being bullied into trouble. Another thing to remember is that, even if you are not good at facial expressions and the person seems to be smiling and apologizing, if these things are being done to you and are upsetting you or getting you into trouble, then you are still being bullied. Here are some of the things that I have experienced at the schools I have been to.

Physical bullying

Physical bullying includes *any* form of unwanted touching at all:

- Kicking, hitting, shoving.
- Pushing out of the line (i.e. the dinner queue) in order to get me into trouble.
- Pushing in front of me in queues so that I am always left at the back.
- Sticking their foot out and tripping me up. I have actually learned how to do a break fall exceptionally well, just by going to school!
- Knocking the dinner tray out of my hand.
- Kicking and prodding through the back of the chair.
- Pulling an odd strand of hair or poking me to make me jump.
- One boy pretended to be friendly (I thought he was being) and talked to me, whilst another crouched down on his hands and knees directly behind me. The lad in

front of me then suddenly pushed me and I fell straight over the other lad and hit my head on the concrete floor. I had concussion.

- Doors being slammed in my face.

Other forms of bullying

- Rulers, pencils and other equipment taken and often being taunted whilst I try to get it back.
- Stuff knocked off my desk so that I get in trouble.
- School books scribbled and drawn on, again so I get in trouble.
- Ink squirted at me, covering my clothes.
- Packed lunch taken and squashed onto the floor.
- Name calling and teasing (these actually don't bother me too much).
- Being deliberately ignored (they call that being sent to Coventry) when I am speaking whilst everyone laughs about it.
- Being left till the end when teams are being picked, or should I say not being picked for any teams!
- Ridiculed for not being good at team sports. I am used to the familiar groan of 'Aw, Sir, do we have to have him?'

I am sure that there are masses more to be added and each of you reading this could add your own.

I feel like I am almost dying of embarrassment whilst I am writing this, but Mum assures me and I have read on the internet that there is another form of bullying…gulp…nervous snigger…this is sexual bullying. I have in *no way* experienced this in any way shape or form but apparently there are lots of people who have. People with AS or any autistic spectrum disorder are vulnerable for many reasons and people can take advantage. Kids may think it is funny to get someone to do rude things. If you are ever told to do something you do not feel comfortable with or someone tries to touch you and you don't want him or her to, then be very clear and tell them to stop it. Phew – my ears and face are so flaming red that I only need to wear an orange jumper and green trousers and I would surely be mistaken for a set of traffic lights!

I will now do a rapid subject change and go on to say that the whole business of bullying works two ways. If you are forcing someone to do something that they don't want, or are hurting someone either by pushing them around or hitting or kicking them or calling them names, then you are being a bully. It may not be easy for an AS person to realize that they are upsetting someone, but that is no excuse.

AS kids may also be trying desperately to fit in and therefore go along with the crowd and join in with bullying others or even start it to make themselves look 'hard'. If you are one of these people, then take it from me, you will regret it. Bullying is wrong. It is not good to hurt other people, physically or mentally.

Adults can be bullied too. If you feel scared and intimidated by someone or they call you names and do anything to you that you don't like, then they are bullying you. I know there are no teachers to tell and I am not too sure what to advise, but if you are in a job and this is happening, then maybe your boss can sort it out. As an adult you can pick who you mix with more, so if this is happening, then just try your best to keep away from those kinds of people.

Teachers can bully too

I hope that I do not get into trouble for writing this. I am sure that lots of teachers are either keen to help those of us who are a bit different, or at the very least are willing to just let us get on with life without hassling us. I have to say though that there are some teachers who seem to be bigger bullies than the kids in the school.

Rachel

I don't mean that these teachers kick and shove and hit anyone, but the things that they do can be just as hurtful, if not more so. Some teachers seem to take great delight in saying things that point out the difficulties of kids like me and then bask in the laughter (metaphorically of course) of the rest of the class. Stuff like raising their eyebrows so exaggeratedly that it is obvious that they are making fun of a person, or calling someone 'thicko' or 'dopey' or other mean words are still forms of bullying. They seem to overcome their annoyance at having someone different in the class by humiliating them. Maybe some teachers are just nasty people. This world seems to have quite a few of those.

The first thing to do if a teacher is picking on you or upsetting you is to tell them very clearly that they are upsetting you. If they ignore you, then you must go and tell the head of your year or the head teacher or even another teacher who you do trust.

Why me?

I must say that it is not just AS kids who are likely to be prone to bullying. People seem to pick on anyone who is different. Those who are fatter or thinner or have a bigger nose or anything else that is not like the majority seem to become the unfortunate victims of the bullies.

AS people have great difficulty with social stuff. There seem to be lots of hidden rules and subtle ways of speaking and behaving that are just impossible to fathom out. Most AS kids don't usually even bother. I know I don't. Difficulties with facial expressions, the use of language and body language all make us targets for ridicule. AS people often have dyspraxia, or at least some difficulties with their motor skills. I don't know many AS kids who like team sports. This makes us stand out even more, as people who are good at team sports seem to be idolized (particularly by teachers) for some strange reason.

I am not too sure why the bullies in my life were so intent on bullying me. I guess because I am different and was an easy target because I was usually alone. I never was quite sure why they bullied me but looking back I think that I was classed as the 'soft' one in the class as opposed to being 'hard'. Apparently the definition of 'hard' is someone who is willing to have a fight with anyone else and beat other people up. I was 'soft' because I never did see the point in that. I still don't. They weren't even fighting over anything in particular!

There seems to be some kind of system for boys at school. AS kids are unlikely to join in with this kind of ridiculous system. Of course this is a good thing but it does make us stand out from the rest of the crowd. This system goes like this 'You lookin' at me?' 'Yeah, what you gonna do about it?' Then follows some hilarious-looking performance similar to an animalistic mating ritual.

Rachel

Both boys stick out their chests and parade around like demented peacocks for a while and then they both mutually agree on a time to meet later in order to go and beat each other senseless with the whole school watching. If a person beats up someone who is 'hard', they earn the title of hard. One thing I have noticed is that if they beat up someone who is a metre shorter than themselves and two years younger, they are still counted as hard. These kinds of kids seem to think (which must be hard for them – most have an IQ of about twelve) that all this is fair. This kind of stuff is beyond my comprehension. The one thing I have noticed in this life is that the world is full of idiots.

I think that this kind of thing goes on as much for girls as for boys, but I have noticed that girls tend to be a lot nastier about each other's appearance and clothes than boys do. Generally, though, I think that adults assume there are far more differences between boys' behaviour and girls' than there actually are. Girls still fight and are just as nasty as boys. Maybe AS girls have a different set of adolescent problems to AS boys – I can't really comment on that – but I do think that our underlying difficulty with communication and understanding is the same.

Another reason I think I have been bullied in the past and am prone to being picked on is that I just don't want to 'run with the pack'. I never have and I never will. I don't see any point in pretending that I like things when I don't. I think this is one of the reasons why other people don't want to make friends with me or hang around with me. They know that if they hang around with me or say they like me, then they too are open to being bullied because of that. I am afraid that I have no solutions to this one as I cannot say to anyone reading this that they should compromise themselves and their beliefs and likes and dislikes in order to be popular. They will end up being unhappier than if they were true to themselves but spent more time alone.

When is a bully not a bully?

I thought of this title when I was thinking of this joke.

> Q: When is a door not a door?

> A: When it's ajar.

Boom, boom! This of course has nothing to do with bullying but I like these plays on words. What I actually did mean is that there is another side to the bullying problem for AS kids – some bullying may not actually be bullying. AS kids don't always realize when friendly messing about is actually friendly stuff. I know this because I have been 'bullied' in the past and Mum has seen and has known for sure that the kid in question was just trying to get me to join in their games. This is where it becomes very difficult so you should always tell someone if you are feeling upset or hurt and leave an adult to have a word with the other person and make him or her realize that you don't like what they are doing. If they really are being friendly, they will understand.

Sometimes the 'bullying' incidents are times when the bullies are play-fighting and having fun and just get a bit rough. That is usually the teacher's argument or excuse anyway! I am not good at telling other people's intentions so that may or may not be true. When a teacher says that, it usually means they are not going to do anything about it. I think it is fine for people to be a bit rough with each other if they all like it, but why involve someone who doesn't? That's when it becomes bullying, I reckon. Whichever way you look at it, I think if someone is getting hurt or upset, then the bullies should stop. I suppose if boys who are not like me enjoy 'battering' each other then they could well be just getting a bit rough. I sure wish they would understand that we are not all the same, though.

There is one kid at school who pushes and shoves me all the time but he has AD/HD so I reckon I should be grown up enough to accept that he has his problems too and that is part of them. I do think it is wrong that his problem gives him a licence to beat people up and people just accept it. I know Mum wouldn't want Joe to be doing things like that.

In general, kids are pretty annoying, but actually as I get older I find that there are a few decent ones around after all. I am not sure whether that is because I have changed or they have changed or it is particular to my new school. Whichever it is, at the time of writing this life is a lot easier in the bullying respect.

Dealing with bullies

A word for parents

Mum used to get annoyed because she said I always left it till the bullying got too much to bear before I told her it was going on. What she doesn't realize is that kids do this kind of thing and I was used to it. Note the use of the past tense here. I am now puffing out my chest (figuratively speaking, of course!) and stating firmly 'no more'. AS kids, if you are reading this bit, then join with me and do the same.

There was another reason for me not telling her things too. AS kids don't realize which things they are supposed to go home and tell. 'What have you done at school today?' wouldn't automatically bring about the answer 'I have been bullied' unless that subject was specifically asked about. I have listed a few bits of advice for parents here, though I am not an expert on parenting or on seeing someone else's point of view. After all, I have AS and…I am only thirteen!

1. If you are asking your child about bullying, then be specific in your questions. You will need to ask if anyone has been pushing or shoving them, upsetting them and being nasty to them or hitting or kicking them. Even then you may not ask the right question so be aware of that.

2. Remember that, as I have said earlier, bullies don't actually say, 'Now I am going to bully you'. Therefore your child may not realize that the torment they are suffering is bullying.

3. One thing that parents should not do is go into school and confront the bullies in front of everyone. All that happens there is that everyone laughs and calls you a

baby and a Mummy's boy and it generally gets even worse.

4.   If you are going to talk to the teachers about your child's bullying, do this in private too. Don't take them into school in the morning and then stop and talk to the teacher. It's not very nice to sit in a class and know that you are being talked about.

5.   When you know that your child is being bullied and you still send them in to school, you are throwing them into a den of lions. It is your job to protect your child so go to any lengths possible to do so.

6.   If it isn't sorted satisfactorily, then please, please, please take your child out of school til it is. Don't make them suffer whilst you try and sort it.

7.   Remember that the option of home education is always there. The law requires someone to be educated at school or otherwise. There are loads of books and further links on this at the back. Even though I am still at school, the security of knowing this is an option makes me feel better than you could ever imagine.

Designer society

I have put this in for parents, because it is the unfortunate parents or grandparents who end up forking out for the clothes, trainers and bags for kids. Nowadays even babies wear designer gear and I do actually think it is all wrong. I am sure that the same pair of jeans that could be bought in some cheapo shop would cost twenty times as much if a designer label was sewn on it. I must say to parents though that, wrong as it is, if at all possible please let your kid have at least some of this stuff.

When Matthew first started senior school, Mum decided she wasn't going to conform and sent him to school with a reasonably priced, ordinary brown anorak. The school phoned up at first break and said that an accident had happened and a load of kids had been picking on Mat and calling him 'earthworm Jim' (now don't laugh!) and ripped his coat. Mum went straight out and bought him a named coat and we have all worn such stuff ever since.

Your AS kids will always stick out like a sore thumb anyway, so try your very best to let them have reasonably trendy stuff if at all possible (if they want it of course) and then you remove one thing that they can be teased about. I know this is hard and I am not the one that pays, but charity shops and jumble sales often sell decent named stuff and you can get some good stuff in sales too. You really don't have to be rolling in it to buy some acceptable gear.

A word for teachers

AS kids, how many times have you plucked up the courage to tell a teacher what is going on, only to find that they either ignore you or tell you to 'stand up to them'? Teachers, I know I am only a kid but here are some ways in which you could help.

1. The most important thing for teachers to know is that being bullied is not simply a part of life that any kid has to deal with (how many times have I heard that?).

2. If a kid is brave enough to approach you and tell you their problems, then please, please take them seriously.

3. Don't announce in class that someone is being bullied. Be discreet, it is embarrassing and leaves us open to even more teasing.

4. Don't tell AS kids that they 'bring it on themselves'. I
    have had that said to me before and I have to say it is
    total...well, I will be polite and say rubbish! Why
    should we have to behave like everyone else just so that
    we don't get picked on? That is *so* unfair!

5. Don't just wander around the yard or look round in class
    and say that you can see no evidence of the bullying. If
    you want to catch them red-handed, then go to some
    dark corner of the yard or sneak to the locker room
    when no one else is about.

6. Most important of all – take it seriously. Bullying equals
    hell! You are the adult and the kids at school are just that
    – kids. You take charge and make it stop in whatever
    way you can. AS kids, and in fact any kids, have a hard
    time in life anyway.

If you are being bullied

Bullies are cowards. I have noticed in my long and very painful
experience with them that, although they act tough in a schoolyard, they immediately break down in tears in a teacher's office.
They seem to know that adults can give out punishments a lot
worse than having them beaten up.

Here are some tips to help deal with this stuff. I know it is hard,
but life is difficult enough to deal with so let your teachers and
parents take care of this. You are not a grass, a dobber or a sneak.
You are just preserving yourself, your property and your sanity,
and quite rightly so.

The first thing to remember is this is *never, ever* your fault.
Repeat after me 'They are the prats and the idiots'. I hesitate to use
the word freak here because that is far too good for a bully!

1. Don't go to a quiet corner somewhere at school breaks. Try to be somewhere safe such as the library. I know it sounds strange but when you think you are hiding you are most likely to be found and bullied. AS kids are not good at working out how other people think. The best thing to do is stay with your friend if you have one, or at least in a place where there are lots of people around.

2. When a pack of bullies – there is always more than one, usually packs with a head wolf – approaches, then just put on a brave face and if at all possible walk away from these situations. 'Is that a flying pig?' I hear you say. (I will spare you the agony of having to go to the back of the book here as this is so important.) People say this when they know that there is no chance of something happening. You see there is no chance of a pig flying either. (OK, OK, AS kids, I know that all this messing with genes may make this possible one day!)

3. When the pack of wolves (I prefer to think of them as a flock of sheep) approaches, and we all know that walking away is usually impossible, try hard to attract an adult's attention quickly. They soon scatter, I can tell you!

4. If you have older brothers or sisters then talk to them. They are more likely to be closer to your level. Your parents are also more likely to listen and accept their word on the subject too. If you have no older siblings then maybe you could try to talk to some older people.

5. If you are being bullied tell a grown-up, teacher or friend that you can trust, tell someone that won't go and tell everyone. Don't be afraid to tell someone. You really *must* do this.

6. Don't push back if they hit or push you. Just walk away because if you hit them back it will only make things worse. Remember, be brave and don't let them see that they are upsetting you. That fuels their fun (sickos that they are!).

7. Try to find out who else is being bullied. Strength in numbers does work.

8. If bullies tease you about something like the way you walk or talk, then try to laugh at yourself and carry on acting as you were before. If you agree with them it is far too much for their tiny brains to fathom and they soon lose their point.

9. It is never, ever your fault. Step back and assess the whole situation and try to find out why it is going on. Find someone you can really trust and tell them everything. Don't hold any details back. Remember this is your life and you don't have to suffer for anyone. Take no crap! Life is too short. If you don't stand up for yourself you will regret it later in life and it will affect you. It will stop. Have faith and courage in yourself and it will get you through.

10. It may be difficult, but be friendly and open and honest with other people than the bullies. The more friends you develop, the more the bullies will leave you alone because people will stick up for you.

One final word about this. Anyone out there being bullied, *don't suffer in silence.* I've been there and done it and, trust me, it's not worth it. These horrible, sad individuals can ruin your life. Some people have even been pushed to suicide through stuff like this. That is very sad and very wrong. Don't let them get away with this stuff. They have the problem, not you, so tell someone and put a stop to it.

If you stay silent and become more scared and depressed, then they win. If we can feel like we are freaks sometimes, if we can rise above being called freaks, if we can make our way through a world that seems to speak a foreign language a lot of the time, then we can deal with half-witted morons who have so little brains that they have to find some other way to pump up their oversized egos.

Remember, the most important thing is to tell someone. It may not be that easy. I know, I've been there! But from my experience I have learned that you can't just sit around and wait for it to stop. You have to do something. If teachers won't listen, then make them. Keep on and on. Go to the head of the school. Get your parents to come in and talk to the teachers. Remember, now is the time for it to stop. From now on, take no more crap!!

11

Taekwondo

It is no mistake that this chapter is straight after the chapter about bullying! Now don't get me wrong. As much as you may feel like it, that doesn't mean that you should learn a martial art so that you can physically get back at the bullies. As far as the bullies of my past are concerned, I like to adopt a 'what goes around comes around' attitude in the hope that at some point those bullies who have made my life so miserable will be on the receiving end. Yes, I know, that's like cursing someone by saying, 'May you lose a small object of sentimental value.' Not very charitable I know, but hey…I can't be perfect all the time!

Now before all of you with AS decide to skip past this chapter because you have dyspraxia or you can't manage crowds, just hang around a moment and read on. I know that you must be rushing to get to the dating chapter but, believe me, learning Taekwondo may increase your chances too! Parents, before you skim over this chapter, presuming that I am going to instruct your kid to learn a deadly weapon which he or she will undoubtedly get into trouble with, read on too and I will show you otherwise.

My Taekwondo class

The association that I am part of is called the ILGI Taekwondo Association. It has loads of clubs in all different areas but Master Waddington is the chief instructor over all of them. He was the one who founded Taekwondo in the North West area of the UK. He is a Sixth Dan instructor who takes the gradings and supervises the instructors of the other ILGI clubs. Il GI is a traditional Korean title which means 'One together', symbolizing a family or group all working together in harmony. Now before you panic and think that this means group work or teamwork, that just isn't true. You are at one with all the other people in the world who do Taekwondo. That's quite a cool concept for me because I am usually alone.

When we started Taekwondo, it was because Joe had a little friend who went there and he nagged and nagged till he was allowed to go too. This is pretty ironic actually because he is the one who messes about and finds it hard. That's because his concentration is so bad and he has such difficulty keeping still. Master

Waddington knows he has these problems and tries to find a balance between telling him off and accepting that he finds it hard. All in all, Joe is doing well I would say. He is only nine after all. If you have AD/HD or your child does, it doesn't mean that they can't do Taekwondo but it may take them a bit longer than most to learn. Have a word with the Master and I am sure they will be helpful.

When we took Joe we found out that the class had all ranges of age and ability so we all decided to join. Matthew stays at home and babysits for, Ben though he does love to learn the moves off us when we get home. Ben has a little Taekwondo suit too. Here are Ben and Mat looking really 'hard'!

I have to say that when we first started I found it so difficult. My co-ordination was terrible and it seemed far worse when I stood with other people who just seemed naturally able. Thanks very much, Ann and Sue, for teaching me and having such patience when I was in the beginners class, and thanks Mum for being as clumsy and unco-ordinated as I am. At least I was not alone!

The history of Taekwondo

Taekwondo, the art of kicking and punching, has a long history of being a self-defence martial art using only the hands and feet to fight off one's assailants. Although the name Taekwondo was first introduced in 1944, the art can be traced back to murals painted on tomb walls dating back to between AD 3 and AD 427.

Although primarily a defensive martial art, it also embodies the principle of defence of the weak. (Now isn't that quite a cool idea? All the 'freaks and the geeks' having the ability to defend the weak!) Throughout the Orient and into India, where in about 3000 BC an Indian prince was recorded as practising killing blows and strikes on his servants, different forms of fighting and defensive techniques have developed. All take various aspects of each other's style and add it to their own particular martial art.

After the liberation of Korea, at the end of the Second World War, there were five main martial arts academies in Korea, all practising Taekwondo but in slightly different ways. These families or styles of Taekwondo are Mooduk Kwan, Jido Kwan, Changmu Kwan, Song Kwan and Chung Do Kwan. At the ILGI Association we follow Chung Do Kwan.

Taekwondo is taught in schools and colleges throughout Korea in much the same way as we would be taught football in this country. (Wouldn't it be cool to live in Korea? Just think, no football!) All military personnel are also required to do basic Taekwondo hand-to-hand fighting in their training. The army has a battalion known as 'The Tiger' consisting of 1000 men – all black belts. As mentioned before, Chung Do Kwan started in 1944 under its first leader and in 1957 Master Kyu Uhm became leader, a position which he still holds to this day. In Korea before 1960, Oh do Kwan – the military section of Chung Do Kwan – was given over to General Choi Hang Hi by Master Uhm and was further developed into the style now practised by the International Taekwondo Federation (ITF).

With the departure of General Choi, the other Korean Kwans (families) formed their own international body that we know as the World Taekwondo Federation (WTF). This style is recognised as being the official South Korean one, having the biggest following worldwide, and is also the style that appears in the Olympic Games.

Wakey, wakey!! I am just checking that all those facts and figures have not sent you to sleep – but then again, most of you will have AS so will probably enjoy it. Personally I like to gather information about as much as possible. Now you know where Taekwondo originated from and what it was used for, you will be probably be even surer that you will not be able to go around knocking people off horseback with flying kicks and serving in the Korean army. Me neither!

Taekwondo uses belts to show the different ranks, ranging from white to black, with yellow, green, blue and red belts in between. After you have done a grading – a series of physical tests and a pattern (more about this later) – you move up to the next 'Kup' grade. I don't know if it is different in any other clubs and other countries, but at the club I go to there is a minimum of three months between each grading until your black belt grading, when you have to wait at least six months to do it. It is often much longer than that as it is up to the Master to ensure that the student is ready physically and mentally before he enters them into the grading.

The first ten gradings are the 'Kup' grades, but it doesn't stop at black belt. After the black belt there are ten more grades (the fun never ends!) and these are called the 'Dan' grades.

As part of every grading, each Taekwondo student executes a series of defending and attaching movements against imaginary opponents. These are performed in a set pattern and are called 'forms' or Poomses. These are really important as they are aimed to develop and enhance essential skills such as balance, timing, co-ordination and breathing technique. In practising these patterns, the Taekwondo student learns to apply the various techniques applicable to their level of development. If you want to and have the skills, then after you are a well-established black belt, ideally a second Dan, you can run your own club – though you have to have the permission of your original master. I know that for a lot of AS people this may seem pie in the sky (now what do you think of that one?!), but there is no reason why we should set our sights lower than anyone else.

The benefits of Taekwondo

Well, now I have bored you silly telling you where it originated from, what you have to do and what it is for, I really should tell you what the benefits are. I do think that I would be writing for a long time if I were to list all the benefits of Taekwondo, but here are some.

How many of you have dyspraxia or at the very least have the co-ordination of a pregnant penguin? Dyspraxia, as I have said, is problems with motor skills. I have this and it means that my co-ordination is very…well, unco-ordinated! I think they call it clumsy child syndrome. Anyway, regardless of whether you have this label or not, if you have problems with co-ordination, judging speed and distance and your own body space, then you will no doubt loathe games and sport as much as I do. On second thoughts no one can loathe games as much as I do!

Within Taekwondo there are set routines and set patterns. At each session there is a set place to stand, a set pattern of stretching and warm-up routines to do and the rules never change from one year to the next. The first few weeks of learning are difficult because obviously, like anything new, these routines have to be learned. After that it's just plain sailing. I don't mean that Taekwondo is easy by any means, it takes work and dedication, but the fact that it is so structured and predictable makes it the perfect form of exercise for anyone on the autistic spectrum.

Even though we are standing in lines and there are lots of people around (which believe me I know can be nerve-racking), in Taekwondo the student must face the front and stand to attention and perform the moves as the Master instructs. That is so cool, because even though we are at one with the rest, we are doing our own thing, putting in our own efforts and working as an individual.

The moves that we do are all designed to sharpen our reactions, improve our co-ordination, increase our awareness of timing and distance and our flexibility. It seems to me that Taekwondo is custom-made for people on the autistic spectrum. The fact that someone is doing physical training a couple of times a week can only be good for them. We do a routine of press-ups, sit-ups, stamina exercises and stretches to increase flexibility. When you first start, these are so tiring. For at least three months I was walking around as if I was one of the riders of the Korean horses, never mind the one performing the kicks! My whole body felt as if it had been used as a punching bag. I'd better not labour this point or I may put you off and I don't want to do that. The benefits are much greater than the inconvenience (not to mention agony!) of a body full of lactic acid. Many, many times I have had to be physically dragged from my computer and shoved out of the door because, as I have said, the computer and the PlayStation seem to consume me (now there is a strange image!). Mum knows though that once I get to Taekwondo I enjoy it and feel better about myself.

Taekwondo (and any martial art) is not just about learning to defend yourself and to punch and kick effectively. It is also about training your inner self to be more aware and more accepting of yourself and those around you. Far Eastern philosophy is something which I find fascinating. The rate of heart attacks, strokes and stress-related diseases is nowhere near as high as in western countries. I think western countries could learn a lot. Sorry to anyone who is from the Far East. I am sure I am preaching to the converted if that is the case!

Tenets are the doctrines or beliefs of a person or school and Taekwondo has its own tenets.

Tenets of Taekwondo

Etiquette Rules of behaviour, showing respect for others.

Modesty Having a humble estimate of one's self, not being boastful or showing off, especially to outsiders.

Self-control Being able to train hard without hurting anyone and being able to control anger or aggression from within.

Perseverance The ability to keep on trying until you master what you set out to do.

Indomitable spirit
To be able to keep on going, no matter how tough things get.

Well, I don't know about you, but I reckon that this is a pretty good philosophy on life. I cannot say that it comes naturally for me to follow them, but like all the rest of you AS people, I need rules and I think that these are a good set of rules for Taekwondo and for life in general.

If you do start Taekwondo and experience that first night panic of 'no way will I ever do this', then all I can say is reread the tenets above and keep trying. Slowly but surely you will feel more able and more confident. It takes time and when you feel like giving up, remind yourself that it will pass. Your master will help you get through the difficult times.

Another thing to remember is that, even though this is a martial art, it is also a way of using your hands and feet as weapons and you never know when you may need that. However good you may be at any other sport, if you are attacked in the street you will never be able to put your tennis or football skills to use to beat off your attacker! I am not saying that you should be using Taekwondo on bullies, but if it comes to a situation where it is either you or them that gets hurt, then make sure that it is them. As I have said before, take no crap!

12

Friendships and Socializing

How to win friends and influence people

Now before any of you go into a strop and start saying that you really don't want to win friends or influence anyone, that, I believe, is an expression. I have already explained to you the fact that I seem unable to think of catchy, snappy chapter titles and sub-headings so if anything vaguely appropriate springs to mind, I am grabbing the bull by the horns!

Again, I have thought carefully about where to put this chapter and it is no mistake that it is before the dating chapter and after the bullying and the Taekwondo chapters. As I have already said, Taekwondo is a great way to feel better about yourself and increase your confidence. It is also a good way to make friends and making friends, I am told, is the first step towards having other kinds of relationships (if you get my meaning...snigger!).

If you are an AS kid and you want to make friends and socialize but don't know how, then I would advise you to do as I have said and just be yourself and try to be friendly, if at all possible. Maybe you could find someone who seems to be a bit of a loner himself or herself and talk to each other. Don't worry too much or get embarrassed when someone gives you 'a look' or an 'evil' (I've been told that's when someone makes a nasty face at you to show they don't like something you've done, or even merely don't like your face!) or tells you off for talking too much or something. This is all part of learning.

I am always being told off for standing too close to people and following them around all the time but it is very difficult to know when it is right to follow someone around and carry on talking and when the conversation has ended and I am to leave them alone. I will never be able to tell if someone is bored unless they tell me, and even then I have to admit that I sometimes carry on talking if it is about my favourite topic. It is easy to know things in theory but not so easy to carry them out.

If you want to blend in with people or find a friend or hang around with someone, then I must give a bit of advice about specialist subjects or favourite topics or obsessions or whatever you like to call them. If you have an overwhelming interest in one topic and that topic is not football, rugby or suchlike, then the sad fact in this life is that it doesn't seem to be acceptable to talk about it to the same extent as if the interest was a common one. Personally I am not bothered at all about running with the pack, but if you don't want to stand out as too different, then that would be my advice. Talking incessantly about one thing leaves us open to bullying and ridicule. Life stinks sometimes! A sad lesson, I reckon, but if we want to get on with people at all, then we too must accept other people's differences as well. I am not sure that I do want to get on with people, actually, but it seems to be easier since I have just accepted myself for who I am, AS and all.

I now have a friend who likes the same kind of things as I do and he doesn't like football or battering people either. As I have said, I like being on my own, but it is also nice now to have a laugh with someone whilst I am at school.

If you have AS then after all you are not the same as others, but that doesn't make you worth any less. I am actually very proud that

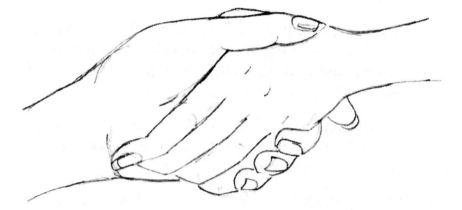

Rachel

I am me. I don't mind my own company at all and have nothing in common with most other boys. This seems to cause teachers a problem. One teacher told me that it was time I stopped being a 'Billy No Mates' and got out there and started having fun. As if his idea of fun was the only way – yeah right! That actually upset me and frustrated me quite a lot. Being alone doesn't. I would say that if you don't want to mix with people and are quite happy on your own, then carry on and don't let anyone push you into anything different.

I am not going to give out tips on how to make friends because I am not good at doing it myself, though I am getting better each day, and you may not want to. Here are a few bits of advice, though, as I say, I am no expert and…I am only thirteen (I bet I am bugging you all with that by now!).

1. If you like being on your own then be happy with your own company and don't let anyone convince you it is wrong.

2. If you desperately want a friend or two then be selective and don't bother trying to be popular by doing things that are alien (groan…I won't repeat the old 'we are aliens' joke again!) to your nature.

3. Try to accept yourself for who you are and all your good points. I have actually started to have people talking to me and now have a friend too.

4. Liking yourself is very important. I don't always like myself and I don't reckon anyone always does but I do try.

5. If you really do want to blend in a bit more then you could make yourself look 'cool'. Get a new haircut, dress in trendy gear (easy to know what that is – just look out for designer labels…ouch – expensive!). This is fine and no problem, *as long as you like it and are comfortable in it.* Never make yourself feel uncomfortable for the sake of fitting in.

I'm not saying that now you will be the life and soul of every party (you never do know), but feeling good about yourself is the first step to getting others to feel good about you. If they don't then hey…it's their loss!!

Just another little word here. If your parents or even school-teachers do try and find you a friend, then as much as it is annoying, it is worth at least attempting to get on with them before you dismiss the idea out of hand. You never know. They may be the perfect match and there is no point in cutting your nose off to spite your face!

A word of warning for pushy parents

First of all the biggest gem of advice I can give on this subject is never to force your child to socialize. Perhaps parents of little, very autistic kids will disagree and that may be a different matter anyway. For kids who are totally locked into their own world I can fully understand why their parents want to give them as much opportunity as possible to notice the world a bit more as possible. I think having other children round in a planned way is one way to try that. For some it may work and for some it may not. I am really talking about AS people here rather than severely autistic people.

Most AS and autistic people are happy just to be by themselves and do their own thing, rather than going out and meeting people and having people around for social occasions. On the contrary, this makes them nervous – at least it does me and other AS people I know. A lot of people with AS also have a problem with crowds so if they are having their 'space invaded' (OK so I couldn't resist this time!) it can at the least make them feel very uncomfortable and at the worst start a panic attack. I used to have panic attacks when I was near crowds. I have always hated crowds. It is a bit like claustrophobia, except instead it's called oclophobia. I discovered all sorts of weird phobias when trying to find out what that was called. Take a look at the links in the back of the book under bullying.

I go to a disabled sport session at Blackpool Sports Centre. It is called Blackpool Bears. It has a range of activities and some people are very serious about sport, whereas others (like me) just mess about. It caters for all ages and disabilities and brothers and sisters go too. There is a bar there which is usually absolutely *seething* with people when Blackpool Bears is on. The first time I went into the bar to buy some chips and a cup of coffee for Mum, I just stared at all the people (there seemed to be millions of them and duplicating by the second) and had what I now know was a 'panic attack'. I just started to cry and got all, well, panicky inside. I was still shaking about half an hour later. It is hard to breathe and I can't help but wring my hands and flap them about when I feel like that. I know I bug my sisters and embarrass them, but I really can't help it. These attacks have actually been eradicated by the GF/CF diet, but there may be different ways to help different people. I am pretty sure that I am not the only one who experiences such things so forcing a situation where this may occur is not good for anyone. I have said loads of times now that people differ, so don't expect your AS child to have panic attacks just because some do.

School is one place where children are expected to be sociable and have friends. It is very difficult for AS kids to have these expectations pushed on them as well as having all the hassles of school to contend with. A lot of kids go to football or Cubs and Scouts or something like that but for me an ideal night in would be to sit and play on the computer or PlayStation or be in my room alone with a good book. My idea of a terrible night is to go out with a group of kids and do activities that seem pretty pointless anyway, like kicking a piece of leather into a net.

I think parents and teachers and adults in general have a big problem with the fact that AS kids like to be alone and don't mix with other people much. My answer to that one is – get over it! Just because one person would feel unhappy or lonely or sad without a crowd of people around them or at least one or two people to chat to, that doesn't mean we have to be all the same. Can any of you parents or adults imagine how you would feel if someone suddenly turned up with a perfect stranger in tow and said, 'You two socialize a bit, I think you might like each other'. Maybe you would be more capable of chatting for a few minutes than an AS person, maybe you would get on like a house on fire, but then again maybe not. I actually reckon that this would be difficult for anyone. If you did manage to overcome your embarrassment and

Rachel

talked to them, only to find out that they were totally different from you, in fact they may as well have come from a different planet, would you still manage to get along with them and enjoy these occasions? Well I don't think so!

If the AS kid wants to have friends but is offending or upsetting people by being too outspoken or interrupting all the time, then maybe you could have little practice times where you show them exaggerated signs of when it is OK to talk and when it is time to listen. Also explain to them things that some people consider to be rude. These are all very hard lessons and certainly not ones that I have got right yet!

If you are a parent of an AS kid or even work with AS kids, then I will repeat myself again and tell you to let them decide for themselves whether they want to socialize or not. If your child is happy on his or her own with their books or computers or chemistry sets or whatever they are into, then leave them alone. I am sure that when they are adults there will be lots of things they will have to do that they really won't want to do. No need to start now!

13

The Dating Game

First, if I even hinted that I had any expertise on the subject of dating, I would be given the title of the world's biggest liar. Hmmm. 'Luke Jackson – the world's biggest liar.' Not exactly the title that I envisaged for myself! I have never asked anyone out in my entire life, although I have wanted to quite a few times. Perhaps by the time of publication this may have changed, but even it that is so, I find it very hard to envisage me turning into some kind of Casanova!

Before any adolescent or teenager is in the unfortunate position of being where I am now, a quivering wreck in the face of certain girls, it seems that all kids go through certain stages from birth to where we are now. I think that there will always be debates about whether boys and girls behave differently to each other because society instils in them these things. Girls are dressed in pink and are given dolls to play with and boys are dressed in blue and given toy guns and cars. Even though not all parents conform to these things, generally that seems to be the way it is. This is where AS kids often differ. We tend to take no notice of these kinds of rules and do our own thing, especially when we are little. My favourite colour was pink when I was little. I certainly didn't care or even know that it was considered 'girly'.

I think society and its way of shaping people and making them conform is rather pathetic. Well actually I think it is *very* pathetic! It seems to me that society as a whole is actually more rigid than AS people. Having an AS kid in the family can actually be very good for the whole family because it surely must make the parents and relatives consider and even revise their whole way of looking at the world. What does it matter if your kid wants to wear pink or carry a doll around? As kids go through nursery and school, they seem to go from playing alongside other kids, girls and boys, quite happily, to actively singling out their own sex and back to mixing with the opposite sex quite happily again. Very strange and, like I said, AS kids do their own thing. We are more likely to be found playing on a computer or lining up cars in a corner than playing cowboys and Indians.

If these kinds of games (which I must admit have always seemed pretty stupid to me) help boys and girls to know more automatically what to do when it comes to dating and boyfriend and girlfriend stuff, then I expect they serve a purpose. I fail to see how they help and maybe they don't, but these are all supposedly natural stages of development that AS kids miss.

At the age of around seven years old or maybe younger, boys and girls seem to kick and push each other a lot. Mum has told me that this is often because they actually like the person they are kicking – and AS kids are considered weird!! AS kids reading this, I am not by any means explaining this so that you think you have to do this kind of stuff. Just be yourself. I am merely highlighting the fact that to get to where we are now – a bag of nerves or a gibbering wreck (these both mean very nervous) in the face of a fanciable person – we have not had the same social experiences as non-AS kids.

Fathom those feelings

Whenever I am within ten metres of anyone that I fancy (I fancy girls but I suppose some may fancy members of their own sex), I feel as if I have suddenly changed from Luke Jackson, the class nerd (which I don't think is too bad), to Luke Jackson, the class cockroach. For some unknown reason, once a girl becomes elevated in a boy's mind (or body!) and takes on the status of a deity, they seem to develop the power to make boys feel extremely inferior just by their mere existence. This is a very different feeling to the usual state of affairs, whereby girls slam doors in your face, call you names and generally treat you like something they would scrape off their shoes – that means dog muck.

I am sure all of you reading this know the kind of girls I mean, and I am even surer that you AS kids reading this experience it frequently. Girls seem particularly cruel, especially when in their packs. Sticks and stones may break my bones, but words can never hurt me. What a load of bullshit (sorry but that is the only word that is appropriate). 'Sugar and spice and all things nice, that's what little girls are made of.' 'Slugs and snails and puppy dog's tails, that's what little boys are made of.' AS kids, if you have never heard these phrases, then they come from a common rhyme and seem to indicate that little boys are made of horrible things and little girls are made of good things. Both you and I know that this is simply *not* true!

When approaching a girl that I fancy, even to say a simple hello, a lot of phrases come to mind immediately. None of them happen literally of course, but when people say that their legs turn to jelly or they get butterflies in their stomach or their tongue sticks to the roof of their mouth, then these phrases become clear when they actually happen to you. When people say that their legs have turned to jelly, they mean that their legs feel weak and shaky. Butterflies in the stomach isn't exactly accurate but it does

Sarah

describe the churning feeling when you are very nervous. I would describe that as more like a rock in a tumble dryer. It's slightly different to that heavy feeling in your stomach that you get when you are feeling very sad. our tongue sticking to the roof of your mouth or being tongue tied is describing the feeling of being incapable of speaking when you know that you really have something to say.

ften when you approach a girl whom you fancy, your face goes red too. With me this happens to my ears. This means that you are feeling embarrassed and I believe it is very natural. I am told that it is nowhere near as obvious to others as it is to you, though somehow I find this hard to believe. When my ears are luminous red, I feel as if I could single handedly (or earedly) light up the classroom in the event of a power failure

AS and dating definitely do not mix. Dating involves a lot of social interaction and I am sure I can also speak for other AS kids too when I say that our reserves are very small. Plus there are not many girls that love talking all day about computers! After a lot of searching, I discovered that there are hardly any tips on dating for quiet kids and kids with AS. I think that this may be purely because it is such a fragile subject. I am now going to rectify this and give out some of the words of wisdom that I have been given myself. Even though I am giving these for kids because I am one, I am sure that they apply to AS people of any age. I don't think this stuff ever gets any easier.

Top tips to enhance your chance

Thanks to my sisters, Rachel, Sarah and Anna for these tips:

1. Shower or bath and wash your hair regularly, probably at least three or four times a week (this depends on how greasy your hair gets). I know this is not likely to be something you want to do, but my sisters assure me that it is important and makes them feel as if you have made an effort.

2. Brush your hair every day and have a decent haircut. Although personalities are important, people are also attracted by appearance.

3. Clean your teeth (I am now sounding like my Mum!) at least every morning and night. My sisters say that there is nothing worse than talking to someone who has slimy teeth and smelly breath.

4. Try to be yourself. Most definitely don't do what a lot of non-AS boys do and act cocky and big-headed.

5. Try to talk to the person's friends and find out what they are interested in.

6. My sisters say that it is good to ask the person's friends if the person in question is actually interested in you as a boyfriend or girlfriend. Personally, I think that they are then likely to go and blab to everyone, so be prepared to cope with this if it happens.

7. If someone asks you outright if you fancy the girl or boy, then don't do as I have done and deny it forcefully, but take a deep breath and tell the truth (and if you are school age, be prepared for everyone to tease you!).

8. If the person you fancy is talking to you, try to listen and not interrupt them.

9. Remember that your specialist subject is not likely to be theirs, so don't talk too much about your fascination. I am told that a good way to judge whether or not it is appropriate to talk about your specialist subject is to answer if they ask questions about it, but not keep bringing it up in conversation yourself.

10. Don't be too serious. Girls like boys who have a sense of humour. My sisters say that it doesn't matter if yours is different to theirs; they still like to see a boy have a laugh.

11. Finally – just take a deep breath and say something like 'Would you like to go to the pictures this weekend?' Remember, faint heart never won a fair lady.

12. Just one last word (OK so the previous wasn't finally!). If you do ask someone and they say no or, even worse, they laugh at you, try your hardest not to let it put you

off. Rejection happens in life and all I can say is 'Pick
yourself up, dust yourself down and start all over again'
(that is from a song).

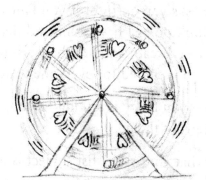

Sarah

The rules of the game – do's and don'ts of dating

More thanks here to my sisters, Rachel, Sarah and Anna:

1. Easy to say and not so easy to do, but try hard to relax.

2. When you first meet the person, try to pay them a
   compliment such as 'You look very pretty', or if it's a
   girl talking to a boy, then you could say something like
   'that shirt suits you'.

3. If the person asks something like 'Does my bum look
   fat?' or even 'I am not sure I like this dress' then that is
   called 'fishing for compliments'. These are very hard
   things to understand, but I am told that instead of being
   completely honest and saying that yes their bum does
   look fat, it is politer to answer with something like

'Don't be daft, you look great'. You are not lying, simply evading an awkward question and complimenting them at the same time. Be economical with the truth!

4. If you are the one who has done the asking for the date, then be prepared to pay for both of you. If the other person insists on paying for themselves then buy them something like a bar of chocolate or a packet of sweets.

5. Don't yawn, stretch and then put your arm around someone. My sisters say that it is better to try to hold the person's hand at first.

6. If you do try to hold the person's hand and they pull it away immediately, it means that they don't want you to do it. If you are unsure, it is best to ask them.

7. If you don't feel comfortable when being touched anywhere on your body or kissed, then simply move away and say, 'I don't feel comfortable with you doing that'. Never feel that you have to put up with something you don't like.

8. Don't fidget by twitching your leg or foot, tapping your fingers, chewing your nails or anything like that. Most girls find this really annoying (don't they Mum?).

9. Remember that the rules for talking to someone you fancy still apply when you are on a date or going out with them. Don't go on about your specialist subject all the time, and listen to them when they speak.

10. At the end of the date don't expect to kiss them. This is a whole new subject and a very difficult one too. If you

have had a good time, then maybe kiss them on the cheek.

11. If the date does work out and you are lucky enough to hold hands or kiss, then don't go talking about it to anyone the day after. If you have a best friend then maybe that would be OK to tell them, but no more. Remember that loose lips sink ships!

12. If the date didn't work out and you didn't get on, then don't stress about this. Try to say goodbye nicely and remain friends.

13. If you really don't want to go out with someone any more, don't let him or her push you into it. Just tell them as kindly as you think you can that you don't want to go out with them any more.

14. A final word about this too. If after one date or even lots, the person you are going out with decides to dump you, then just accept that is their decision and up to them. Don't take it as a personal insult. Some people just don't get on.

I know that I am only thirteen, have AS myself and may not seem qualified to write such tips, but then again people often write about subjects they haven't personally experienced. I must say a big thank you to my brothers and sisters for their advice and I know that I for one plan to implement some of these tips as soon as possible – wish me luck!!

14

Morals and Principles – Representation and Reality

One of the reasons I have written this book is so that people can know what life is really like for a person with AS – in particular a young person. I also wanted to dispel any misconceptions about AS and people on the autistic spectrum. It seems to me that young people and teenagers in particular get a real bad deal. All those teenagers in agreement say 'Ay'! British laws are so strange that they don't give any guidelines to teenagers as to when they are considered 'grown up'. I am afraid I do not know anything about the laws of other countries, but I am sure that anyone reading this will be able to think of similar ambiguities in their laws.

I have not reached these ages yet, but my sister and brother have. You can have sex at sixteen years old but need to ask a parent's permission to get married before you are eighteen. You can smoke at sixteen but cannot go into pubs or buy alcohol til you are eighteen. This doesn't apply to me and maybe other AS kids in quite the same way, but for social people like my sister, it does make me wonder what they are meant to do from the age of sixteen to eighteen – sit at home and smoke and have sex?

If a crowd of teenagers goes into a shop, then the shopkeeper is automatically on his guard, suspecting them as potential shoplifters. If a group of boys goes to a football match then the police are wary of them, expecting them to be football hooligans.

Joseph

Matthew says that in nightclubs the bouncers often turn away a group of lads for no reason as they think they are likely to start fights. Matthew has a car now and has been stopped for random checks so many times. Mum has never been stopped and Matthew is doing nothing wrong. I am sure that is because of his age. Teenagers have a bad reputation and I for one think a lot of it is unjust. I and lots of other kids are in the tricky situation of not only being a teenager or adolescent, but also being a 'freak' too.

At one time I don't think anyone had really heard of AS and there needed to be some publicity and some way of making the world in general more aware that all those 'nerds' and 'freaks' that people come across at school and in the workplace could quite easily be people with AS who are misunderstood. Nowadays there is more awareness of autism (note that I didn't say understanding), but still I think that people only get glimpses of AS and what it actually means.

I must say that not everyone even wants to understand and there will always be some people who enjoy teasing and making a laughing stock out of those who are different. After all it is said that a leopard cannot change its spots (there are two for you to turn to the back for here!).

Negative publicity

One of the worries about telling anyone that I have AS is that it may be regarded as a mental illness. Sorry anyone who is reading this that is mentally ill or knows someone who is – I don't mean it in a bad way at all, quite the opposite! People who are mentally ill get an even worse deal than people with AS, I reckon. I am sure there are lots of people who don't agree with me and everyone has their own opinions. That is just mine and after all…I am only thirteen so maybe it might change one day. The reason I think this is that when I watch the news or see programmes about people with schizophrenia and other problems, it is always about really negative stuff that they have done. Mentally ill people are usually portrayed as those who go around stabbing people for no apparent reason and generally committing awful crimes. Sometimes there follows a debate on how society has failed them because they lived on the streets or whatever, and I am sure it has, but I am also sure that not all mentally ill people go around committing such crimes. Publicity about the cases that do happen understandably makes people who don't understand very worried. After all, no one wants to be stabbed for no reason. Come to think of it, I don't think anybody would like to be stabbed *for* a reason!

With these problems and lots of others like AS, autism and AD/HD, there needs to be more teaching about this kind of stuff so that everyone is more aware. I also wonder whether people that are labelled as schizophrenic or other things are actually on the autistic spectrum and no one has understood them properly. I don't know a lot about schizophrenia or other mental illnesses but I can imagine how adults that have gone all their lives confused and misunderstood would seem as if they had a severe mental illness. I am sure it would cause depression too.

Mum says that when I was younger and used to scream and kick and throw things about, it could have been because she didn't know why and so wasn't helping. She says that, looking back, she could have been changing my routines without knowing it and exposing me to horrible sensory experiences and all that made me go wild. I just can't imagine how awful it would be to feel like that for a whole lifetime. I think I would be locked away somewhere myself! These are just my thoughts and after all (here again is my copout) I am only thirteen.

The media are full of negative stuff. The national news very rarely publicizes good stuff. It is all about muggings and rapes and murders and burglary. That's just the way it is, though personally I think we would all be a lot happier if people's social chitchat (not that I engage in social chitchat, but I know that kids, AS or otherwise, have to hang around whilst their parents do...groan!) consisted of 'Did you see that amazing person on the news today?' rather than the usual 'Wasn't that awful on the news today?' I wonder whether the media only show all the bad stuff because that is what the world wants, or does the world only talk about such stuff because that's what the media portray? Which came first, the chicken or the egg? Because of this fascination for morbid and negative stuff, naturally when an AS person commits a crime it hits the news and AS gets bad publicity. We are all then tarred with the same brush (go to the back!).

Rules are not made to be broken

It's possible that a lot of people think that whenever a person with AS commits a crime it is because AS people are more prone to criminality. I don't consider that to be true at all. In fact it is rather insulting…in fact it is *very* insulting! How many of you AS kids get called a 'swat' or a 'keen bean' or a 'spiff'? I know I have many times. That's because we are able to follow rules and even like having such rules. Contrary to popular agreement, rules are *not* made to be broken. I just follow them because…I can't really say why. I guess it makes me feel secure. We are rigid in our thinking by nature. AS is a lifelong set of behaviours so there is no reason at all why someone should hit adulthood (whenever that may be) and suddenly develop a dislike for rules. That is just not logical.

A general conception of AS is that AS people have difficulty understanding how other people feel and think – well that is true to a certain degree. Now I can only guess that the opinion that AS people are more likely to commit crimes is based on the assumption that we are incapable of recognizing that this will hurt and upset other people. Although there may be AS people who have committed crime, generally, and certainly with me, it is the opposite of this. Some people may presume that an AS person thinks, 'The law says that I am not allowed to break into people's houses, but hey they have something I haven't got so I will do it anyway.' Wrong! An AS person is more likely to think, 'The law says I can't break into a house so I won't do it.' We like rules. Rules make things easier to understand. Rules are clear. Rules are *secure*. AS people are a lot more rigid in their thoughts than other people.

I hope I am not misunderstood here and not taken to be saying that AS people will do everything everyone tells them. I can most definitely tell when something is a rule that is made for the good of others and me and when there is a kind of 'rule' going around amongst school kids or maybe even older people. I have to say, though, that I haven't always been able to tell a good rule from a bad rule and I am sure a lot of AS kids have difficulty with this. Adults, that's where you come in. It's up to you to explain these things clearly to the AS kid.

If someone told me to try a cigarette, it definitely doesn't mean that I would do it. The one thing I hate most is smoking. The only reason the government has not banned it is because they get more money from cigarette tax than from anything else. People die all the time from lung cancer and emphysema and other diseases that are related to cigarettes. People of my age smoke because they think it looks 'hard', when in reality it is not 'hard' at all to be a sheep and not be able to say no to something that is bad for you and the rest of the world. I don't think AS people who knew all the facts about smoking would smoke at all. Our lungs were hardly designed to be coated in tar! I would like to think that we see things more for what they are than what they look like.

Joseph

The same can be said of other people trying to entice you into committing some crime like stealing or shoplifting. Although most teenagers are not bad, they do tend to go around in packs and it seems like points are scored for who is the most daring, regardless of the rights and wrongs of what they are doing. I am going to carry on being a 'wimp' and refuse point-blank to shoplift, take drugs or smoke. I may drink when I am older, but only in moderation, though I suppose I may get drunk one day. I am only thirteen (or have I not told you yet?...sarcasm) so I cannot say much about that at the moment.

So when you are called a freak and a wimp and a nerd or a geek for not taking a cigarette or shoplifting, just smile to yourself and think, 'Hey, I'm not the one who is going to get lung cancer or go to a juvenile delinquent centre' and carry on with what you are doing. If you are going to get any friends, it won't be the ones who expect you to do things that are wrong. Friends just accept you for who you are – weirdness and all!

Moral musings for adolescent Aspergers

1. First things first. Remember that you have AS and therefore you are different. Different is cool. Not more stupid, not uglier, not less funny – purely and simply different. Think how boring life would be if everyone thought, looked and acted the same!

2. Don't think that because you have AS or other difficulties you are superior to others without it. Prejudice works both ways.

3. A golden rule that is actually from the Bible is 'do to others as you would have done to yourself'. I know it is self-explanatory but if you are unsure, it means don't do anything to anyone else that you wouldn't like to have done to yourself. A good rule I reckon.

4.   Don't try to do *anything* that doesn't come naturally to you in order to gain popularity or cover up for your difficulties.

5.   Don't let anyone pressure you into having sex or anything like that if you are not ready or old enough to. Remember that the UK says you have to be at least sixteen. I am not sure about other countries. That doesn't mean that you must do it as soon as you reach the age of consent. It doesn't matter if you are a lot older.

6.   Remember that even one illegal drug can kill you. Don't *ever* be talked into trying such things.

7.   Remember that nicotine is more addictive than heroin and if you do try one cigarette you may like it and not be able to stop. Have the strength to *say no!*

We should also remember that no one can just take what he or she wants because, although some things may be better, there would be complete chaos in the long run. Some people would be greedy and take too much so people would go hungry because of it. Things would run out quicker; people would take lots and lots of everything so things like fossil fuels would run out faster. That is why the whole world is in such a state. People in some countries are dying of starvation whilst in other countries people are dying of heart attacks due to overeating. The world is very unevenly balanced, full of powerful people and governments wanting to own countries and have great power over others.

I had better finish this chapter by getting off my high horse and explaining that I am by no means perfect (my brothers and sisters will all be nodding vigorously in agreement as I am typing this). I would hate all you AS kids to think that I am some goody,

goody who merely pontificates over world problems. Sometimes I do things that I really shouldn't do and then I am mad at myself. Sometimes I do things that I shouldn't do and then I am mad because I have been caught! I am not at all perfect and I do tell lies and I do 'steal' things out of the cupboard occasionally. I really don't think that is the same as being prone to crime. I wouldn't dream of breaking the law and I do know that others would be hurt and wouldn't want that. The only thing I do is take biscuits out of the cupboard and then pretend I haven't so that I don't get into trouble. Sometimes the temptation is too great and there is nothing I like better than shutting my bedroom door, switching on my lava lamp and fibre optics and settling down with a book and a packet of biscuits. Of course I should really be sleeping then, so I have just given myself away! I have to say that I have even done this with biscuits that are not GF/CF, which causes a whole new set of other problems because then I can't stop craving gluten and casein again and it is very hard to resist the craving. Generally though, it is GF/CF foods that I take.

15

One Final and Positive Note

Have I made any of you feel less freakish? Have I made you at least realize that you are not alone? If so, this book is a job well done. Stand up and pat yourself on the back, Luke Jackson. Oops…a little lapse in my modesty there! This book has been a strange one for me to write and as informative for me as I hope it is for you readers. There I was, writing about the games I played in junior school and trying to inform parents about how an AS child thinks when – wham!! – hormones hit me like a truck hurtling down a busy lane, whilst all I could do was freeze to the spot like a startled rabbit. I have to admit though that, weird as it is, confusing as it is, I am kind of liking this new-found me – some days at least. Other days I yearn for the security of my balaclava or my pencils.

This may apply to non-AS teenagers as well as AS teenagers. I don't know about you, but some days I wake and feel quite grown up and well on my way to adulthood, whilst other days I feel very young and silly. Mum often says I have got out of bed on the wrong side (mine is up against a wall!) and it's hard to control those kinds of moods. They just overtake me. I have to say that I am nowhere near as bad as Sarah who would easily win the world's moodiest teenager award if one were to be handed out (sorry Sarah, lovely as you are, you know it is true!).

Isn't it annoying that most people remember the film *Rain Man* when anyone mentions autism and Asperger Syndrome? For those of you who don't know (though I am sure that is not many), the film showed the AS guy performing astounding feats like saying the exact number of matches and cards dropped before they even hit the ground. There have also been programmes featuring a man who played the piano brilliantly without ever being taught and another lad who had the most amazing ability to draw buildings in perfect detail after he had only seen them once. This is fantastic stuff, but these people are called 'savant autistics' and are very rare in comparison to the masses of us who are either below, above or average in our abilities.

I don't know about any of you AS readers, but I found those programmes depressing. It seems that I have got the nerdiness and the freakishness but none of the genius! Wouldn't it be cool to be able to show off some amazing talent like that to all the girls...sighs. A boy can dream! These programmes also make Joe Public think we should all have some seemingly supernatural ability and that is not at all helpful. Parents please don't expect your autistic or AS kid to suddenly burst forth with such talent. They just may not have any phenomenal talents but that makes them no less a person than a 'savant'. We are all amazing in our own way. I have to say here that the attitude that AS people are somehow superior to non-AS people seems as prejudiced and wrong as the attitude that AS people are somehow inferior because they are different.

All you AS people reading this, remember that just as you want people to accept and try to understand you and your AS, you too should accept and try to understand other people's differences. They can't help it if they don't understand you. It's up to us to teach people. What non-AS people *can* help is not even trying to understand us and presuming that, because we are a minority, we are inferior. That is *very* wrong. The things my sister does and says and the way she acts are odd and alien to me, but yet I accept that her idea of fun and mine and her way of understanding things and mine are completely different. Neither one is better or worse than the other. Mum says it is intolerance and unwillingness to learn about difference that is the bad thing. Wise words!

Both you and I know that some people are just not interested in understanding and really get their kicks out of having someone to pick on. The world has got a lot of bad people in it but also a lot of good people. Personally, I think there are more good than bad. Try to be positive and focus on the good bits and when you are weary and fed up with being misunderstood and misunderstanding, then mentally allocate yourself a treat. Get through the day and chill out in the way that is best for you. I go on the PlayStation or read a book. When it is warmer, I go outside onto our trampoline. We have a full sized one with a massive net around and I often just bounce around or lie there and let the cares of the day fall through to the ground like autumn leaves. Whatever works for you then do it. You need to devise your own personal defrag.

Sometimes I just come home from school or get out of bed and stand very still and look at one thing in particular. People without an autistic spectrum disorder often busy themselves with everyday life and don't seem to notice the detail in our world. One phrase that I heard on an advert, but which is actually by William Henry Davies (1871–1940) is: 'What is life, so full of care, if we have no time to stop and stare.' I often do just that – stop and stare. Buildings are fascinating, plants and trees are fascinating – so many different shapes, aspects and angles all used to make one whole. Just staring at the same piece of flooring for any length of time can produce a different image with each squint of the eye and turn of the head.

I realize that this can sometimes be a problem, especially when you are trying to concentrate on something very hard. You notice different things around you and your attention wanders. This is especially annoying in lessons or in an exam and then it is good to find ways to block the fascination out of your sight so that you can focus on the task. All in all though, this is definitely one of the things I like best about myself and AS.

This teenage thing has made me recognize the world around me a bit more, especially certain members of the world. Whilst the adolescent rituals are unattainable and unattractive to me, I am getting better at fitting in. Well actually I must admit that these feelings change from day to day. Sometimes I even question my diagnosis and wonder if it is wrong, but then other days I really do feel like the world's biggest freak! In fact, I have gone from thinking about computers ninety nine per cent of the time to only thinking about them ninety seven per cent of the time. Can you guess what I am thinking of the rest of the time?

I have tried to be very positive throughout this book and I truly believe that the key to inner peace (doesn't that sound hippyish – yeah man!) is to be aware of yourself, both your strengths and your weaknesses. I wouldn't be honest if I didn't say that I do get fed up with having to try so hard, so often I just take time out. I lock myself away into my world of computers and then arguments still arise because Mum says it is not healthy to be so obsessive about any one thing. She may be right, she probably is right, but at the moment that's the way I am. I never did profess to be perfect and after all…I am only thirteen!

All I can say to end my book (and give you one last hysterical mental image) is that whatever you are doing, believe in yourself, keep your nose to the grindstone and your head above water. If you find yourself sinking then stop, take a breather and remember, it isn't over until the fat lady sings!

Idioms – an Explanation

A lick and a promise.
> A half-hearted effort.

Being economical with the truth.
> Not being completely honest.

Bear with me.
> Be tolerant.

Bark is worse than their bite.
> When someone sounds angry but they are really quite kind.

Better to have loved and lost (than to have never loved).
> It makes you a better person if you have loved at all, even for only a short time.

Call a spade a spade.
> To speak plainly – to describe something as it really is. It has been in use since 300 BC and pre-dates the slang use of the term 'spade' meaning 'African'.

Catch-22. Joseph Heller's novel. It was all about how anyone who applied to get out of military service on the grounds of insanity was behaving rationally and thus couldn't be insane.

Cut your nose off to spite your face.
> Disadvantage oneself to annoy or do harm to someone else.

Don't cry over spilled milk.
> No point in worrying about what has already past.

Face like thunder.
>To have a very angry expression on one's face.

Feeling under the weather.
>To feel ill.

Fishing for compliments.
>Trying to entice someone into paying you compliments.

Forking out for.
>Pay money for.

Getting the sack.
>Being told to leave one's job.

Grasshopper mind.
>This means that a person's mind jumps from one subject to another in a few seconds.

Get off your high horse.
>Do not act like you are superior to everyone else.

Get out of bed on the wrong side.
>Get off to a bad start or be grouchy and grumpy.

Getting on like a house on fire.
>To like each other a lot and become friends very quickly.

Grabbing the bull by the horns.
>Be firm and take control.

Hand on heart.
>In all honesty.

In my heart of hearts.
>Deep inside yourself.

It isn't over till the fat lady sings.
>It isn't over until you are sure it is over.

It never rains but it pours.
>   When trouble comes, it comes in doubles.

Keep your nose to the grindstone.
>   Concentrate on working hard. This came from the fact that knife grinders in Sheffield lay on their fronts with their noses towards the grindstones.

Keep your head above water.
>   Stay on top of things.

Labour the point.
>   Go on and on about a subject.

Laughing stock.
>   The butt of all the jokes (my brother Joe will think that's funny, he is always saying 'kiss my butt').

Leopard never changes its spots.
>   Some people never change.

Loose lips sink ships.
>   An Allied slogan during World War Two meaning unguarded talk may give information to the enemy.

Many hands make light work.
>   A lot of people working together help make things work.

More than one way to skin a cat.
>   There are many ways to do things.

On cloud nine.
>   To be very happy.

On the tip of my tongue.
>   Almost able to recall.

Plain sailing.
>   Extremely easy.

Pie in the sky.
> An impossible dream.

Pigs might fly.
> No chance of something happening.

Rolling in it.
> To be rich.

Setting the ball rolling.
> To start off the work.

Stick out like a sore thumb.
> Look out of place.

Take a breather.
> Have a rest.

Teaching your Granny to suck eggs.
> Telling something to someone who already knows a lot more about it then you do.

The ball is in your court.
> When someone has to make a decision for themselves before any progress can be made.

Throwing a wobbly.
> To suddenly become very angry.

Too many cooks spoil the broth.
> This means that, although working together is OK, too many people may spoil it.

Why have a dog and bark yourself?
> Why do something yourself when you can get someone else to do it?

Further Reading

Attwood, T. (1998) *Asperger's Syndrome: A Guide for Parents and Professionals*. London: Jessica Kingsley Publishers.

Blakemore-Brown, L. (2001) *Reweaving the Autistic Tapestry: Autism, Asperger Syndrome and ADHD*. London: Jessica Kingsley Publishers.

Cumine, V., Leach, J. and Stevenson G. (1999) *Asperger Syndrome: A Practical Guide for Teachers*. London: David Fulton.

Cumine, V., Leach, J. and Stevenson, G. (2000) *Autism in the Early Years: A Practical Guide*. London: David Fulton.

Dowty, T. and Cowlishaw, K. (2001) *Home Educating Our Autistic Spectrum Children: Paths are Made by Walking*. London: Jessica Kingsley Publishers

Fullerton, A., Stratton, J., Coyne, P. and Gray, C. (1996) *High Functioning Adolescents and Young adults with Autism: A Teacher's Guide*. Austin, TX: PRO-ED.

Grandin, T. (1995) *Thinking in Pictures and other Reports of my Life with Autism*. New York: Vintage Books.

Hall, K. (2000) *Asperger Syndrome, the Universe and Everything*. London: Jessica Kingsley Publishers.

Hansen, M. and Hansen, J. (1998) *E is for Additives*. London: HarperCollins.

Holliday Willey, L. (1999) *Pretending to be Normal: Living with Asperger Syndrome*. London: Jessica Kingsley Publishers.

Jackson, L. (2001) *A User Guide to the GF/CF Diet for Autism, Asperger Syndrome and AD/HD.* London: Jessica Kinsgley Publishers.

Le Breton, M. (2001) *Diet Intervention and Autism: Implementing the Gluten Free and Casein Free Diet for Autistic Children and Adults.* London: Jessica Kingsley Publishers.

Lewis, L. (1999) *Special Diets for Special Kids.* TX: Future Horizons (distributed in the UK and Europe by Jessica Kingsley Publishers)

Martin, J.M. (2000) *Complete Candida Yeast Guide Book.* London: Prima.

Seroussi, K. (2000) *Unravelling the Mystery of Autism and Pervasive Developmental Disorder: A Mother's Story of Research and Recovery.* New York: Simon & Schuster.

Useful Addresses and Websites

Useful Addresses

Autism and Asperger Syndrome

Asperger Syndrome Coalition of the US
ASC-US, Inc.
PO Box 49267
Jacksonville Beach
FL 32240-9267
USA
Tel: 866 4ASPRGR or 866 427 7747

Autism Society of America
7910 Woodmont Avenue
Suite 300
Bethesda
MD 20814-3015
USA
Tel: 800 3AUTISM or 301 657 0881

Education Otherwise
PO Box 7420
London N9 9SG
Tel: 0870 7300074

Home Education Advisory Service (HEAS)
PO Box 98
Welwyn Garden City
Herts AL8 6AN
Tel/Fax: 01707 371854

National Autistic Society
393 City Road
London EC1V 1NG
Tel: 020 7833 2299
 Fax: 020 7833 9666

Dietary and medical

Allergy Induced Autism (AiA)
11 Larklands
Longthorpe
Peter PE3 6II
Tel: 01733 331771

Alternative Therapy Network
1120 Royal Palm Beach
Blvd. 283
Royal Palm Beach
FL 33411
USA

Autism Research Unit
School of Sciences (Health)
University of Sunderland
Sunderland SR2 7EE UK
Tel: 0191 510 8922
Fax: 0191 510 8922

Feingold Association of the USA
127 E. Main Street # 106
Riverhead
NY 11901
USA
Tel: 631 369 9340

Hyperactive Children Support Group (HACSG)
71 Whyke Lane
Chichester
West Sussex PO19 2LD
Tel: 01903 725182
Fax: 01903 734726

International Health Foundation
PO Box 3494
Jackson
TN 38303
USA
Tel: 901 427 8100
Fax: 901 423 5402
A range of information and books available relating to allergy and
nutritional approaches to ADD and ADHD.

Websites

Autism, Asperger Syndrome and AD/HD website links

www.add.org/
National Attention Deficit Disorder Association.

www.autism.org/stories.html
A website all about social stories. Just have a look!

www.dyspraxiafoundation.org.uk/
Dyspraxia foundation. All the information needed about dyspraxia.

www.hyperlexia.org
Information and more links about hyperlexia (the precocious ability to read at an early age).

www.isn.net/~jypsy/
Oops! Wrong Planet! Syndrome - Asperger Syndrome page with masses of links and information.

www.melbourne.citysearch.com.au/E/V/MELBO/0073/33/3 9/4.html
Website of the Irlen dyslexia centre.

www.members.tripod.com/~Rsaffran/index.html
All about applied behavioural analysis (ABA).

www.ocfoundation.org/
Obsessive compulsive disorder foundation website.

www.oneworld.org/autism_uk/index.html
National Autistic Society.

www.pyramidproducts.com/
Link to the Picture Exchange Communication System (PECS) website.

www.tonyattwood.com/
Tony Attwood's homepage with lots of information about all aspects of Asperger Syndrome. You really *must* read Paper 4 about homework!

www.trainland.triapod.com/
A site with Winnie the Pooh backdrops, loads of links, PECS pictures and loads of educational stuff.

Home education website links

www.education-otherwise.org/
Another home education link.

www.he-special.org.uk
Home education link for the UK.

HE-SPECIAL-UK@yahoogroups.com
An internet-based support group for those home educating or having school problems.

Bullying website links

www.bullying.co.uk/index.html
A UK website with all sorts of advice and support about bullying.

www.ilgitaekwondo.co.uk/
The website of the Taekwondo club that I attend.

www.kukkiwon.or.kr
The headquarters of the World Taekwondo Federation.

www.successunlimited.co.uk/
A site that has all the links you could ever need to do with bullying.

www.theappleaday.co.uk
This has links about bullying, health and fitness, phobias and all sorts of other stuff. It's a bit cheesy but very informative!

Diet and medical website links

www.autism.com/ari/
The Autistic Research Institute in San Diego. Information about recent research into autism. Organizers of DAN (Defeat Autism Now) conferences.

www.autismmedical.com
The allergy induced autism website with useful links and forum.

www.feingold.org
All about the Feingold diet for the USA and worldwide.

www.gfcfkids@yahoogroups.com
A worldwide internet-based support group aimed at those implementing the GF/CF diet anywhere in the world.

www.gfcfkidsuk@yahoogroups.com
A UK-based internet group aimed at those implementing the GF/CF diet and other forms of biomedical intervention.

www.osiris.sunderland.ac.uk/autism/
The website of the Autism Research Unit containing the Sunderland Protocol: a logical sequencing of biomedical interventions.

Index

negative thoughts 92–3
nicotine 186
Nintendo 48
noise
  distinguishing between
    foreground and background
    65
  hypersensitivity to 17, 73–4, 113
  and sleep 95
normal, appearing 24
nystagmus (wobbly eyes) 69, 81

obsessions 21, 43–59, 191
obsessive compulsive disorder 55
occupational therapists 115
oclophobia 167
Oh do Kwan 158
oil burner 93
Olympic Games 158
operations 80
opposite sex
  dating 170–8
  fancying 172–4
  making friends with 83
  talking to 39, 175, 177
organizing 50, 55
ownership of property, rules about
  112

panic attacks 167, 168
parasite problems 84
parents
  advice to 29, 42, 56, 59, 60, 68,
    120, 122

  on bullying at school 148–9
  sleeping solutions 94–8
  need to be precise 109–12
  telling children they have AS
    30–42
  warning to, on socializing 167–9
patterns and shapes, fascination with
  64
paying for a date 177
PECS (picture exchange system)
  57–8
pedanticism 22
pencils 51–2, 57
peptides 82, 83, 85
perception, different 69
perseverance 161
phobias 167
physiology, different 77–85
pineal gland 81
play-fighting 146
PlayStation 18, 44, 48–9, 104,
  126, 161, 168, 190
Pokémon 44, 48, 121
politeness 100–1
popularity, avoid doing things for
  sake of 186
precision in language 109–12, 114,
  115
prescription drugs 93
pressure 66–9, 95, 97
principles *see* morals and principles
probiotics 84
problem-solving 50
professionals, helping understanding
  of 14, 28, 60